P9-EMP-571

799.124
BII2
BAB
Babb, James R.
Crosscurrents

DATE DUE

8/06

DISCARD

PUBLIC LIBRARY
EAST LONGMEADOW MASS.
01028

CROSSCURRENTS

Crosscurrents

A FLY FISHER'S PROGRESS

JAMES R. BABB

Foreword by Ted Leeson

THE LYONS PRESS

Copyright © 1999 by James R. Babb

All Rights Reserved. No part of this book may be reproduced in any manner whatsoever without the express written consent of the publisher, except in the case of brief excerpts in critical reviews and articles. All inquiries should be addressed to: The Lyons Press, 123 West 18 Street, New York, NY 10011.

799.124
B112

Printed in the United States of America

Library of Congress Cataloging-in-Publication Data

Babb, James R.
    Crosscurrents : a fly fisher's progress / James R. Babb: foreword by Ted Leeson.
    p. cm.
    Based on the author's columns written for Gray's sporting journal.
    ISBN 1-55821-946-3 (hc.)
    1. Fly fishing Anecdotes.   2. Babb, James R.   I. Title.
SH456.824   1999   99-29607
                                                          CIP

APR 1 9 2000

10-23

For Linda,

who has kept me laughing for
twenty-six years and counting

Contents

Acknowledgments

*T*hanking all the people who help turn raw thought into a finished book can become as ridiculously rambling as an Oscar-acceptance speech and just about as annoying, so I'll keep this short.

Thanks first and foremost to my pal Ted Leeson, who in addition to his embarrassingly fine foreword provided both the idea and the encouragement for a book grown out of my angling columns for *Gray's Sporting Journal*. Thanks Ted. I couldn't—and wouldn't—have done it without you.

Thanks to David Foster and Leslie Nelson, my co-conspirators at *Gray's,* and to my wife Linda, who cares nothing at all about fly fishing but who has always been my most valued and valuable editor, and my best friend.

Thanks to Nick Lyons, who has been at various times a competitor, a mentor, an employer, my publisher, and the only person other than my mother who ever telephoned to say hi on Christmas morning.

And thanks especially to the fish and the rivers, and to my father, who taught me to care about them.

Foreword

*F*or most of us fly fishing is the exception rather than the rule, a respite tucked into nooks and crannies of time, a brief reprieve spent in the small eddies and calms that occasionally form along the edges of a busy world. But a rare and lucky few somehow manage a life that joins avocation with vocation and makes angling both a recreation and a livelihood. James R. Babb—Jim— is a passionate fly angler and for several years now, as editor and angling columnist for *Gray's Sporting Journal,* a professional one. For readers, this union of fly fisherman with writer could not be more fortunate. Jim marries a lifetime of angling skill and experience to an astonishingly (at times alarmingly) fertile imagination, and the offspring is this remarkable collection of stories and essays—brilliantly entertaining and outrageously distinctive and both for the very same reason: a kind of storytelling that pops you upright like a jolt of raw moonshine.

What rings on every page of this book is a tremendously energetic, expressive, and robust voice. It is, sometimes by turns and sometimes all at once, completely irreverent and savagely funny, astute and engaging, eccentric, shrewd, chronically witty, both plainspoken and eloquent, thoughtful, earthy, and extravagant. Imagine for a moment a book coauthored by Charles Dickens and Flannery O'Connor, then edited by Hunter S. Thompson, and you might get some idea of this voice. Its evocations of people and places are vibrant with the texture and vigor of locality; few writers have such ear for the accent, the rhythm, the picturesque vividness of regional speech. The accounts of the fish and fishing, from the quiet solitude of a brook trout stream to the barely controlled chaos of saltwater angling, are immediate and fresh. At times the voice is stropped with an edge as keen as life, laying open thoughts or impressions that tingle like nerve endings. At other times it can barrel down on you with the headlong locomotive energy of a fast freight train careering down a mountainside—not merely unstoppable, but quite possibly dangerous. Always, though, it surprises—in the unexpected clash of images, in striking turns of phrase, in a completely anarchic sense of irony and humor, in disparate ideas rubbed together that magically catch fire. It is distinctive and original, an authentic voice, pure homegrown.

It could not be otherwise, for we write who we are. The words are stamped with the temperament, disposition, and personality of the writer. And like the voice in this book, Babb is doggedly independent and unconventional, a "different drummer," as Thoreau puts it (a man, by the way, with whom Babb shares more than passing similarities). He's pursued a path defined by principles and interests fundamentally his own; often as not that's an uphill walk, traveling, as he says in the central essay of this collection, "Against the Grain." And when the thrust of an individual life bucks the momentum of Life, the collision is bound to produce some strange twists, eccentric deflections, a quirky flux and counterflux.

Growing up in a small East Tennessee town and eventually chafing against its small-town provincialism, Babb moved north, a hillbilly with dreadlocks and a beard who married into Boston's cultural elite where, he says, "I learned to navigate the silverware." He left with a head full of Marley and Mozart and moved farther north, working for a time as a self-employed commercial lobster-man and then jumping ship to become a book editor for a small nautical publisher soon snapped up by a Fortune 500 company. His most distinguished achievement in postsecondary education, he'll happily tell you, was graduating first in his class at the Ryder Trac-tor Trailer Training Institute. At the same time, his appetite for books has always been voracious, and he's read more of them, and understood them better, than most university English professors I know. In the woods of coastal Maine, he built a house entirely by hand, a "Hobbit-like" structure as he describes it, a minor monu-ment to energy efficiency, low-impact living, ecological harmony, and self-reliance; he lives there with his wife, Linda, largely through the forbearance of the three cats who actually run the place. Sequestered in a separate little cabin at the edge of a trout pond (both of which he also built), a charmingly secluded and Waldenesque setting, he works in the publishing business, one of the most public and visible of all human occupations. Deeply mis-trustful of technology, a man who regards flush toilets as an ultra-right-wing conspiracy, he is a sucker for electronic gadgetry—a Luddite with a laptop, Thoreau with a GPS and fax machine.

These are the crosscurrents and paradoxical trajectories of a life, and because the teller cannot be separated from his tale, they are as much a part of this book as the fishing.

But in the end a book, like a trout stream, is most fundamentally shaped by what lies beneath the surface, and at the bottom of this one are places—certainly places with fish in them, but also those places that through birth or occupancy or affection we lay claim to and call our own, and that in time stake their own claims and come to possess us. Connections of this sort can grow deep and complex; locality and family, land and livelihood, home and history twist and vine together until, like it or not or both, who you are and where you came from become very much the same question. Personal identity and place intertwine so deeply that they cannot be teased apart.

Nor should they be. Their union has been a wellspring for Southern writers ever since there was a South, and it is the taproot of this book as well, anchoring its chapters as they unfold to reveal a distinct private geography. Sometimes explicitly, often more subtly, these pieces weave together the story of one man leaving the South, parting from home and home water and better than two centuries of family history. Eventually homesteading in Maine, the author finds both a new life and an even older past: 350 years earlier, one Philip Babb left his own family in England to homestead this very same coast, earn his living in the fishing trade, and lead by necessity the same self-sufficient life that the author has adopted by choice. And as ancestral Babbs would eventually strike out for Tennessee, so Jim Babb branches out to new territory and discovers once again echoes of home. It is a wonderful and strange genealogical déjà vu where the past waits around every bend, sometimes with a Christmas turkey and sometimes a rubber hose.

The one constant throughout this story is fishing, linking the past to the future, the waters that haunt to the ones that beckon. As always, the catching can be good or not, but the angling in these pages never fails to interest and entertain, sometimes provoke and exasperate, and occasionally outrage. For I might as well warn you now: Babb is a writer for whom practically nothing is sacred, nothing to be taken too seriously. Not fishing, not fisherman, and most especially not himself.

—Ted Leeson
February 1999

An Apology

No life, my honest scholar, no life so happy and so pleasant as the life of a well-governed angler; for when the lawyer is swallowed up with business, the statesman in preventing or contriving plots, then we sit on cowslip banks, hear the birds sing, and possess ourselves in as much quietness as these silent silver streams, which we now see glide so quietly by us.

—IZAAK WALTON, *The Compleat Angler*

Oh my. Another collection of navel-gazing essays from a baby boomer who got hold of a fly rod and a word processor and thought Eureka, I've found myself. And now wants to share.

In a dozen years spent as an acquiring editor for a couple of book publishers and now for *Gray's Sporting Journal*, I've rejected enough introspective fly-fishing essays to fill the body of a ten-wheel dump truck and edited enough to fill the cab. Some were good, some were bad, and a rare few made me want to take up golf. But many left me thinking, Yegods, another one. Which makes me more than a little uncomfortable about foisting off on the reading public a fly-fishing collection of my own.

I can't begin to justify this, not really, except to offer the feeble excuse that fishermen fish and writers write, and as I am by default both a fisherman and a writer I can no more resist this course than the one that dictates I sleep, eat, and excrete. Certainly I didn't choose to become a fly fisherman, no more than I chose to be born with blond hair and blue eyes and unhealthy appetites for fried chicken and what is known in polite circles as low humor.

My father was a fly fisherman, and if my brother and I wanted to spend any time with him we had to become fly fishermen, too. My earliest memories all involve fly fishing: Sitting waist-deep in a riffle with my brother, Walter, and Beth Orrin in front of the Orrins' cabin on East Tennessee's Tellico River, watching the evening sun turn our fathers' fly lines to fluorescent candy canes flashing through the moist mountain air. Heaving a dehooked Scarlet Ibis toward backyard quoit-ring targets using the mighty two-handed roundhouse swing of a scrawny three-foot kid with a nine-foot cane rod. Tweezing tiny bluegills from the riprap around Fort Loudoun Lake with miniature Gaines poppers while wearing a coonskin hat and a Red Ryder six-shooter. Warping that heavy cane rod into half a parentheses on a giant doughball-sipping carp that didn't even look back when it dragged me off a footbridge.

I write about fly fishing because I don't really know how to do much else, and like all writers I must write about what I know and about how I live my life. To burgle an appropriate line from Thoreau's introduction to *Walden,* "I should not talk so much about myself if there were anybody else whom I knew as well. Unfortunately, I am confined to this theme by the narrowness of my experience."

The compulsion to write is more easily quelled than the compulsion that sends me looking for good holding water even in big-city storm gutters. I write because I can, I suppose, or more accurately I write because the U.S. Navy's radioman school taught me to type fast enough to keep abreast of an uncontrolled thought process that, like fly fishing, transports me to places I never expected to be.

I write because it is an outlet, a safety valve that may keep me from devolving into that hoppity little old man on the adjacent airplane seat who delivers a six-hour stream-of-consciousness monologue about an unbearably uninteresting subject. But as this particular monologue is about fly fishing, I have to presume it's a subject at least nominally interesting to you.

And, well, I write because some of those navel-gazing fly-fishing essays are among my very favorite books in an extensive and eclectic library—books by a Leeson or a Gierach, a Thomas or a Barsness, a Lyons or a Norman, a McClane or a Maclean are as well read and dog-eared and as meaningful to me as their equally well read shelf-mates tagged Twain and Thoreau, Melville and McCarthy, or Poe and Pynchon: Great Literature, at least to those whose worlds revolve around fish and the places they live.

Everyone has to aspire to something, and while I have too much of the mountain mountebank in my makeup to aspire to anything like greatness, I hope at least to make someone smile now and then.

Fly fishing, I have learned in forty-something years of obsessing over it, is simply too much fun to be taken seriously.

I

Taking a Set

*That's hit, by golly! Now why the devil can't I
'splain myself like yu? I ladles out my words at
randum, like a calf kickin at yaller-jackids; yu
jis' rolls em out tu the pint, like a feller a-layin
bricks—every one fits.*

—GEORGE WASHINGTON HARRIS,
*Sut Lovingood. Yarns Spun by a Nat'ral Born
Durn'd Fool.*

*W*hatever else I may be—husband, father, reader, writer,
editor, sailor, gardener, amateur chef, fly fisherman, environ-
mentalist, ex-smoker, ex-commercial fisherman, ex-truck driver,
lapsed guitar player, apolitical agnostic, bipedal omnivorous mammal—I am first and foremost an East Tennesseean. I say this even
though I have lived more than half my fifty years in Maine and
left East Tennessee behind at the age of seventeen.

But being an East Tennesseean is not something you ever stop
being, no matter how long you've been away.

We are not like other people, us East Tennesseeans. We are not even like other Tennesseeans; the bluegrass Democrats from Middle Tennessee and the Deep South denizens of West Tennessee share in common with the ridge-running Republicans of East Tennessee only a state capital, a license plate, and one star on the three-star flag that officially proclaims our separate and always capitalized identities. We are endlessly friendly, endlessly giving, endlessly neighborly, endlessly contradictory, endlessly unpredictable. We are what Thomas Wolfe, a mountain-grown North Carolinian sprouted from the same gnarled Appalachian roots, described as a "crude, kindly, ignorant, and murderous people."

In my hometown, as typical an East Tennessee village as exists, murders were almost unknown but killings about as common as hookworms and pellagra. If you're wondering about the distinction, a murder is when a wife catches her husband with her sister and blows them both away, or when a footpad slices a bootlegger's throat for the fat wad of tobacco-scented twenties stuffed in his hogwashers. A killing takes place in a beer joint on a Friday or Saturday night, and is inevitably preceded by the most chilling words you can hear south of Mason and Dixon's line: "Whut're *yew* lookin' at?" Of a town a few miles from my own, novelist Cormac McCarthy wrote in *The Orchard Keeper:* "I never knowed such a place for meanness."

I say all this because I've found, over thirty-odd years of life among both urban and rural Yankees, to whom East Tennesseeans are but a minor subspecies of generically caricatured knee-slapping Southerners and East Tennessee only the home of the Smoky Mountains and Dolly Parton, that this usually helps them understand why I am as I am. And at least in part why I don't live in East Tennessee.

Like many Southerners with literary inclinations, I needed to grow distant from my roots before I could look back and truly see them—the deafening contradictions of folks unselfishly opening their hearts and homes to longtime neighbors and newcomers alike, then crushing them with scurrilous embroideries of half-truths and lies whispered down party lines; of unlocked doors and safely strolling late-night streets, and killings and drunken rages and blind superstition and third-world health care; of cherubic Sunday School voices belting out Red and yellow black and white being precious in His sight, and those same voices the next day chanting Two-four-six-eight we don't wanna integrate. For those who could not reconcile such seraphic Sunday lessons with the weekday's harsh hypocrisy, the Old South—where, as Faulkner wrote, "the past isn't dead, it isn't even past"—could be an untenable place.

Thirty-something years in the North.

And yet . . . and yet when I think of naked intolerance, economic apartheid, and willful parochial ignorance I think not of the South but of the North, where I have seen far more pale illiterate faces twisted with hate toward people about whom nothing more is known beyond their percentage of epidermal melanin than I ever saw in the South. And when I think of home it is not wild romantic Maine that makes me go all teary-eyed but East Tennessee, where in its ripe red clay and fissured limestone my roots intertwine deep and ancient.

We are not like other people, us East Tennesseeans. But we are very much like each other. Our defining characteristic: Although we feel things deeply and passionately, there is simply nothing in life so grim or so serious that we can't make fun of it. We make fun of each other and we make fun of ourselves, at every stage of life and beyond. The most laughter you will ever hear is at an East Tennessee funeral, where the dearly departed's myriad foibles are trotted out and gleefully gnawed over with our aggressively informal and outwardly illiterate language, so liberally peppered with grotesqueries and wild exaggerations.

In East Tennessee a handkerchief becomes a snotrag, a washcloth a warshrag; the delicately titillating Northern expression Don't get your panties in a bunch, becomes Don't getchee drawers in a wad. Minor insults are later related with "I could just have *kilt* him"; trivial embarrassments with "I could just have *died.*" When it's blistering hot in Maine and the thermometer's climbing toward triple figures, Mainers will say, "It's a dite wahm t'day." On the same day in East Tennessee, we'd say, "Hit's hotter'n four-hunnerd HAILS out chere." We delight most in inflicting these homespun crudities on the pretentious and refined, all the while smiling and exuding the openhearted good cheer of the idiots they suppose us to be, as we methodically go about turning their blue blood and pale faces an honest shade of red. And this cuts straight across social and educational strata.

On our first visit home, my Northern-born wife and I were eating country ham and biscuits and redeye gravy in a glossy hillbilly-theme restaurant squeezed into the tawdry strip-mall and fireworks supermarket that sucked the life from our once cozy little downtown. As Linda struggled with the concepts that country ham is actually supposed to taste like a pig-flavored salt block and that grits aren't actually food but a kind of spackle formulated to plug up fork tines long enough to convey redeye gravy and pepper from plate to mouth, one of my father's old fishing buddies walked over in his patched jeans and fish-scaly flannel shirt to say howdy: "Hail, Jemmy. Ain't seen you in a coon's age. Whar you been at?" We talked on through the stream-of-consciousness web of fishing stories laced with the weird and distorted that typify an East Tennessee conversation, reminiscing about fish caught and fish lost and various horrors witnessed or perpetrated. After he left Linda asked, "Yegods. Who was that halfwit?" "Him? Oh, he's a nuclear engineer, works over in Oak Ridge designing reactors and stuff."

We drove around my little town, its once homogenous population of intermarried cousins now swollen with Yankee-transplant bedroom commuters zipping up the interstate to Important Jobs in Knoxville. I showed Linda where I was raised, where I worshiped, where I went to school, where I learned to fish, drink, smoke Camels, and fight. I showed her the small-town library tucked into a corner of the War Memorial gymnasium, where I learned about worlds where people talked and thought differently, worlds where anyone could sit by the river and read an unassigned book without someone suspiciously asking Why. I took her to an old friend's house for supper, where we told wild stories of the old days and pored through our high school yearbooks trying to remember who was related to whom: "Lessee, he was my second cousin out of the Chamberlains, so would that make him your fourth cousin on your meemaw's side or your third cousin on your father's side?"

We told stories of the local characters—of Tumor Irwin, a gotch-eyed construction worker with a goiter on his neck the size of a banana squash who lived in the woods in the backseat of a car, the front seat being stored with the car dealer who sold him a newer one every four years and who once tried to sell him a Hudson, renowned for its backseat if not its reliability, and to which offer nondriving half-blind Tumor replied in guttural disgust: "Sheeee-it. I wudden have a goddam Hudson." Of the shadowy early-morning mirages of osteoporotic Old Lady Satterfield and her towering microcephalic son Peehead, fist-fighting with possums for the back-alley contents of well-to-do trash cans. Of Eggs-Worth-of-Candy, heading for the OK Grocery to trade a single hen's egg for a scant jawful of peppermint drops. Of Mutt Wilson, a man of few intelligible words who, after watching the three Click Brothers struggle to erect the giant seasonal Santa Claus atop the Guy F. Tallent Mortuary, strode purposefully to the middle of

Broadway and hollered "Up on the Rooftop, Click Click Click." Of Buzzard Neeley, a professional gambler who'd bet a week's pay on which bird would fly first from a telephone wire and would usually win. Of my great-uncle Flea, a tiny active man fidgeting on the bench at Spit-and-Whittle Corner with overall-wearing men named Barlow and Fiddlehead, trading lies and knives and 'mater plants and mules and peeling stobs of red cedar into nests of fragrant shavings to receive their 'baccer juice. Of Lambseye Dailey, an itinerant odd-jobster and barrelhouse piano player of clouded optics who, when riding shotgun with my dad in the milk truck he once drove, responded to the simple question, "Anythang comin' your way, Lambseye?" by answering, "Nuthin' but a couple of mules," and neglecting to mention the mules were riding in a five-ton truck. Of an old man down the road in Sweetwater who when asked why he dragged a chain with him everywhere said he'd look like a damned fool trying to push it.

Back in Maine, I overheard Linda on the phone describing the trip to her sister: "I used to think there was nobody else in the world like him. But my God, there's *thousands* of them down there."

I knew, not long after moving north in the late 1960s and trial-floating my Jethro Bodine accent past the unapproving ears of Proper Bostonians, that my upbringing was a bit out of the cultural mainstream and needed some sprucing up to be presentable in polite society, but I didn't find out my fly-fishing education was equally askew until a year or so ago when Leeson and I were exchanging letters about this nascent book's raisin deeter, as they say in France. "Even given your advanced age," he'd written with the cheek of someone six years on the sunny side of fifty, "tunnel-fishing tiny streams with cane rods and wet flies wouldn't exactly be considered standard practice for the day." And, he pointed out, my fly-fishing novitiate wasn't exactly "in the Maclean vein—dry flies on four-count beats on classic water for big fish."

No. Maclean it weren't, if for no reasons other than we were Methodists, which rock-ribbed Presbyterian Maclean characterized as "Baptists who can read," and you can't cast on a four-count beat if you're draped over a downed sycamore and sidearming a pair of wet flies two pockets upstream through a doglegged hole in the rhododendrons. Dry flies? In those pre-genetic-hackle days they were hard to keep afloat in the wild mountain torrent; and, as my dad said, they were awful hard to sink deep enough to catch a fish. And big fish? A fourteen-incher was a good trout for us, which is probably why in my hormonally addled adolescence I lit off for the Tennessee River to drift shad guts for catfish the size of Labrador retrievers.

But the skills learned on those little high-mountain streams have worked for me pretty much everywhere I've fished, while skills learned on classic waters don't transplant into the mountains worth a dip of snuff. A case in point: A noted fly-fishing author was in East Tennessee fishing the South Holston—one of the country's great tailwater fisheries—for highly selective, pig-fat trout, and where a big fly is a size 18 and a stout leader reads 6X. While we were talking over the editing of his latest book, I suggested he might like to get together downstate with my brother and do a little mountain fishing. A few weeks later I called Walter and asked how it went. "Well," he said. "I dropped him off on the best pool on the river and said he should fish upstream about two miles and we'd meet at the truck for lunch, and when he didn't show up I walked back downstream to see how he was doing and he was still standing in the same pool using a fly so small you couldn't even see it: 'I'm working one over here against this logjam,' he'd said. 'I got him to rise twice, but I'm having trouble with microdrag.'"

"What'd you do?" I asked. And Walter, who'd fished his two miles of river upstream from the truck with a weighted nymph and a wet-fly dropper and had caught thirty or so trout, and had walked back downstream another two miles to see if his guest had fallen in the river and drowned, during which time his guest hadn't moved ten feet and was fishing a twenty-foot leader on a thirty-foot-wide boulder-strewn stream roaring wildly down a mountainside, said: "I let him fish. I mean, he'd written some of the best books ever on fly fishing. Who the hell was I to tell him you cain't catch fish that way up here?"

The fish stories in this section all take place in East Tennessee, or have their roots in East Tennessee. But then the same could be said of all the stories in this book or of any story I've ever told or am ever likely to tell, for although I have lived in Maine most of my adult life, I really left East Tennessee only in a corporeal sense. That's enough for the folks down home, though, for I found, like everyone who leaves home, that life grows different in your absence and you grow different, too, while to home-folks your life was frozen in amber the day you headed off to the world beyond. To them you'll never grow up, no matter how old you get or what disparate paths your life may take.

A few years back, on a trip home to see my mother and brother, a new interest in family history led me to the old Babb homeplace and burying ground out at Oral, the improbably named village where my great-great-great-grandfather Hiram settled after moving down from Greene County in 1810. I hadn't been there since the 1960s, when on a trip home from Boston my parents had dragged me by—all long hair and attitude and that sneering condescension peculiar to newly sophisticated country bumpkins and to young people who spend time only with people just like themselves.

I stopped at the store to ask directions. "I think it's just off Eblen's Cave Road," I told the stooped old lady behind the Grape Nehi sign, "but I don't remember just where." She squinted suspiciously at my Maine plates and Yankeefied accent, looked me up and down with rheumy eyes, shook her head twice as though to clear it, then finally said: "Whale, yew got the *look* of a Babb, but I cain't tell whether you're bricklayin' Babb or bass-singin' Babb."

"I'm bricklaying Babb's grandson and bass-singing Babb's son," I said.

"Oh," she said with her own brand of condescension, "That'd make yew hair-growin' Babb."

1

Specks in Time

The mountains were his masters. They rimmed in life. They were the cup of reality, beyond growth, beyond struggle and death.

—THOMAS WOLFE, *Look Homeward, Angel*

They're old, these mountains. Some three hundred million years before the Grand Tetons even needed a training bra they towered over the supercontinent Pangaea. As time wore on they sagged slowly into the continental midriff, and today their eroded remnants stretch in long, parallel folds from the Gaspé to Alabama, their steep wooded slopes the East's last wild refuge against the human tide flowing in from the coast.

When a mile-thick sheet of ice covered North America as far down as the Ohio River, these mountains provided a different kind of refuge, high ground in a frozen flood. Northern pine, spruce, and hemlock crowded onto their shoulders, and the thousands of snowmelt streams that cut to the sea teemed with a primitive char scientists call *Salvelinus fontinalis* and Northern anglers call brook trout. Down South, at the coccyx of the Appalachian spine, they're known simply as specks.

Speckled trout evolved with the earliest glaciers, and they and their first cousins, the Arctic char, still live only in the coldest and clearest of water. When the glaciers retreated and the land grew warm, the specks sought sanctuary in the high country, in the cool mountain streams that drain the closest thing to a rain forest in eastern North America. A foot of elevation equals just over a quarter mile of northing, and at around thirty-five hundred feet above sea level the brook trout of southern Appalachia live, phytogeographically speaking, in the cold comfort of Maine.

And as the last glaciers retreated humans pushed into these mountains, hunting mastodon and caribou and, archaeologists tell us, fishing for specks. When Abraham wandered forth from Ur and Khufu began his pyramid, new people moved into these mountains and, in the fertile river valleys and deep mountain coves, began a rudimentary form of farming. By the time a minor Saxon tribe named Babba first entered the Teign River Valley of what is now Devon, England, an elaborate agricultural civilization lived in and around these mountains; it ended shortly after 1541, when Hernando de Soto's band of gold-hungry brigands barged through, leaving behind disease and desolation and a vacant niche for a fiercely independent Iroquoian semimatriarchy known as the Cherokee.

In the eighteenth century the American-born sons of European settlers began moving into these mountains, including the descendants of one Phillip Babb, who in 1650 left England for Isles of Shoals, Maine, where he was Magistrate and Fishing Master, a buyer and drier of codfish to be shipped back to London, as his grandfather and father had done since the 1580s from the waters off Newfoundland. From Babb's Cove on Appledore Island, a lonely blasted rock nine miles out at sea, the thin green coastline of Maine and New Hampshire spreads from horizon to horizon, and behind it the ancient stubs of the blue Appalachians dominate the sky as they have for eons. In years to come the five sons of Phillip Babb would move into those mountains, some going north, others south.

In 1787 great-grandson Philip Babb left his father's plantation on Babb's Run, a thin little trout stream notched into the Blue Ridge Mountains of Virginia, for the wilds of what would become Greene County, Tennessee. He ran a mill on Babb Creek, a thin mossy rill slicing through the limestone of Bays Mountain toward Roaring Fork and Lick Creek.

After he returned to Greene County from the siege of York-town, Philip's son Seth opened his own mill and started a family. Later, his son Hiram moved south into the lonely hill country between the Tennessee and Clinch Rivers, where he built a two-story log house whose front porch still overlooks the Cumberlands and its back the Great Smokies.

Fish brought my family to America, and I like to imagine a different fish and the mountains they lived in played a part in drawing Philip and Seth and Seth's son Hiram and Hiram's son Isaac ever farther into the Appalachians, searching for a home in the kind of wild, pure country where speckled trout live. I like to think I am genetically encoded to need the feel of those mountains and those pure speckled trout always nearby, and that this is what sent me north from East Tennessee a quarter century past to live in Maine, at the opposite end of the Appalachians and in the epicenter of the brook trout's range. I know genetic encoding is what continues to take me back regularly to the streams my family has fished for two hundred years, to the streams and the mountains where I grew up and learned to fish, always searching for this canary-in-a-cage indicator of what is still wild and pure in my native land.

*　　*　　*

It is May and the trout lilies are blooming, and like Southern mountain people for centuries we have taken this as a sign to go fishing for specks. We are my brother, Walter, and his friend Richard Blackburn; they have fished the streams in these mountains almost daily for four decades and know them as well as anyone alive. We're about thirty-seven hundred feet above sea level, having driven up the steep, winding dirt road the forest service graded over the old wagon trail that led from the Davis Settlement to the Green Cove Store, where my father shopped for bacon and beans and horehound candy back in 1924 as a twelve-year-old Boy Scout. We're planning to fish Meadow Branch, a tributary of North River, which is a tributary of the Tellico River, itself a tributary of the Little Tennessee River, the sacred river of the Cherokee, now imprisoned behind a series of implacable concrete dams and on whose banks once stood the Cherokee town from which Tennessee got its name.

The Tellico is managed as a put-and-take fishery for rainbows, a haven for PowerBaiters intent on catching their limits right after the Saturday-morning opening and being back in Tellico Plains at Hardee's by seven-thirty, eating sausage biscuits and thinking they've been trout fishing. But the Tellico's tributaries are managed as wild streams—no stocking, three-fish limits, artificial lures only—and the fishing is good, sometimes great, for streamborn rainbows and browns and, up high, in some streams, for specks.

In a few hours of fishing between violent spring cloudbursts, we release some thirty specks from six to nine inches—good fishing by 1990s standards. But these aren't pure Appalachian brook trout, a newly named subspecies diverted from the mainstream gene pool by a million years of glacially imposed isolation. These Meadow

Branch brookies are of mixed parentage, native Appalachian specks mingled with northern hatchery stock, the result of a well-intentioned a-brook-trout's-a-brook-trout attempt, beginning fifty years ago, to right a wrong perpetrated some twenty years before.

In the teens and twenties, low-geared Shay locomotives of the Babcock and Little River logging companies began creeping down out of these mountains along spidery trestles and rough-laid tracks, trundling to the sawmills a virgin forest that covered an area the size of England and leaving behind a blasted landscape. With the tight forest canopy gone, waters warmed and filled with eroded topsoil, killing environmentally sensitive specks by the millions. To mollify public opinion, the logging companies began stocking Sierra Mountain rainbows; train crews tossed in milk cans full of them at every river crossing.

Before the log-off my father's fishing buddies Floyd King and Billy Gilbert came up into these mountains on horseback and found good fishing for specks fourteen inches or better down to sixteen hundred feet. Below eight hundred feet lived native smallmouths and redeyes; in the waters between lived only horny-head chubs. The rainbows and, later, browns initially colonized this vacant niche, but as their numbers grew the rainbows expanded upstream, and as usually happens with introduced exotics the newcomers took over, driving the few surviving specks high into the thin, infertile trickles. Soon, like the Cherokee and their predecessors, the once plentiful Appalachian brook trout had virtually vanished from its native land.

When I grew up fishing here in the 1950s and 1960s, all the streams were heavily stocked, and a six-inch wild speck in a creel full of twelve-inch hatchery-bred northern brookies, rainbows, and browns was a great prize. An aesthete might attribute this to the true Appalachian speck's beauty and rarity, but in those pre-catch-and-release days we prized wild specks for the same reasons the mountain people do today: They taste better than any fish that swims. I know old-timers who wouldn't walk across the street to catch a twenty-inch brown or rainbow but will crawl through miles of nearly impenetrable rhododendron thickets for a mess of sardine-size specks. Served alongside fried pokeweed and the fierce wild leek we call ramps *(Allium tricoccum)*, a plateful of specks is the true and inseparable core of an Appalachian Spring, Aaron Copland notwithstanding. Alas for a threatened species, elevation to culinary totemhood by a hardy, hungry, enterprising, and not particularly law-abiding populace can be a dangerous thing indeed.

I had wanted to fish Sycamore Creek—a Tellico River tributary that to me defines the perfect trout stream: no more than thirty feet wide, with icy crystalline water stair-stepping over big mossy boulders, its steep intimate banks shaded by towering beech and tulip poplar and frosted with trilliums and lady's slippers—the kind of idyllic oasis that sends the "Flower Duet" from Delibes's *Lakme* endlessly lilting through my head. But Walter had already scouted Sycamore Creek, and this year we had come too late.

Sycamore Creek's once plentiful jewel-bright wild browns and rainbows are being purged to make way for Appalachian-strain specks imported from Great Smoky Mountains National Park, their pure genes protected from further alien infection by a new and theoretically impregnable concrete prophylactic built just upstream from the main-river junction. Sycamore Creek is a well-publicized keynote stream in the state's brook trout restoration program, inaccessible except at its mouth near the fish hatchery on the Tellico River, or at its upper end by those who know how to cut cross-country from newly and unnecessarily constructed Highway 165 between Tellico Plains, Tennessee, and Robbinsville, North Carolina: the Road to Nowhere, meant to bring economic prosperity by reasons still unclear to a region interminably unprosperous. But as I drive along the ridgelines and pull into the officially sanctioned scenic overlooks, I see no prosperity in this road. All I see is fast-food effluvia and malt-liquor cans tossed from whizzing cars and acid leaching from blasted ledgerock into once pristine headwater streams. I see habitat destruction and backdoor access to areas better left inaccessible.

In its wisdom, the state of Tennessee has fewer game wardens on the job hereabouts than forty years ago, when the state's population was less than half what it is today—game wardens who have neither the time nor the inclination to bivouac deep in these mountains in hopes of catching a slick brook trout poacher who knows the country far better than they do and who almost certainly holds their lives pretty cheap.

On his scouting visit to Sycamore Creek the previous week, Walter didn't find any fish over three or four inches, but at the upper end he found a fire ring full of trout heads and ramp leaves and a gallon-size Ziploc bulging with rotting specks—a sizable chunk of a slim gene pool dropped by a poacher with his arms full.

The following day we fished high up on the headwaters of Bald River, where only pure mountain-strain specks live, protected behind a natural barrier of steep stair-step falls and a tangled hell of interlocking rhododendrons and trees downed in a massive ice storm that struck the high country a few years ago.

Even here, after a six-mile trudge likely to deflect even the most ardent of today's soft city trout fishers, shiny RC cans and Copenhagen boxes tell of recent visitors who knew the area and knew what they were doing; the stream held only a few fish over five inches, at least for us.

I wanted quasi-scientific proof that fish of some kind still lived in these mountains and had not all died out in the freakish wrathful weather of the past few years, so we headed over the mountain to a stream whose name I'll not share and caught the living bee-jezus out of wild, never-seen-a-hatchery rainbows, six of which got suitably Babbtized in popping bacon grease and served up with a skilletful of fat ramps we'd dug up above forty-four hundred feet on Mud Gap—our own family Rite of Spring. They weren't specks, but by God they were good. And the stream that produced them was fully as inaccessible as Sycamore Creek or the Upper Bald River.

What saved it from poachers? It has no speckled trout. What saved Meadow Branch's naturalized Yankee specks from poachers? It runs right alongside a forest service road patrolled by the cell-phone-equipped Guardian Angels branch of Trout Unlimited—city boys from Chattanooga, for the most part, who discovered this wild stream a few years back in the Post-Movie fly-fishing craze and who mean to guard it from interlopers, at least until some old-timer from Rafter or Coker Creek blows one of their fly-bespeck-led-hat-wearing heads off.

"Locals are locals," says Steve Moore between mouthfuls of barbe-cue. He should know. Like me, he is one—born and raised just across the mountain in North Carolina from where we're eating lunch, outside the Tennessee-side entrance to Great Smoky Mountains National Park. He's also the National Park Service fisheries biologist in charge of restoring brook trout to the park and, increasingly rare in these days of bureaucratic disconnect from the resources they're meant to protect, an ardent fly fisherman.

"They'll get some of them," Steve says. "But they'll never get 'em all. But I don't have to tell you: Up here, brook trout are part of the heritage, like moonshine. And we want to get brook trout to the point where they can be fished again."

They're heading in the right direction, it seems. In the seventy-five years since the big log-off, the lands within the national park are well into regrowth, and after brook trout populations hit a low ebb in the 1950s, current distribution is roughly the same as in the 1970s, about 45 percent below the 1930s survey by Willis King—not exactly prospering, but no longer losing ground.

Some evidence even suggests that brook trout are reclaiming waters on their own. Stream pH levels are increasing, in part because the maturing forest's soil has higher nitrate levels than it did when new growth dominated the area after the log-off; large trees, with their deeper roots, take up fewer surface nutrients than small trees, and the residue washes into the streams. It may be that as the forest matures and stream pH naturally rises, specks will gradually move downstream and displace rainbows, a fine bit of fair-play turnabout.

No one knows for sure why introduced rainbows were able to outcompete native brook trout in these mountains; in the West, the opposite is often true. Brookies and rainbows are both opportunistic fish, both the products of thin waters. On paper brook trout should dominate, as they have larger mouths than rainbows—a ten-inch brook trout can handily swallow a frog half its size while a rainbow cannot—and they are generally more efficient feeders. In the great drought of 1988, for instance, rainbows here lost weight throughout the season while brook trout either gained weight or stayed the same.

Size for size, a brook trout is just as aggressive as a rainbow, but the rainbows spearheading the upstream invasion invariably were the largest fish in the stream, and the steady upward pressure from fertile waters teeming with fish into which ever more were stocked inevitably won out over the feeble remnant speck populations reared in the thin highland trickles.

To fully recover, the specks need a hand. Eighteen park streams with natural barriers are targeted for full brook-trout restoration, meaning the rainbows will be shocked and transplanted elsewhere and, if necessary, their waters restocked with Appalachian-strain specks taken from nearby streams.

I mention to Steve that some longtime local trout fishermen worry the park service and the Tennessee Wildlife Resources Agency will go too far, urged on by the Shiite wing of the cold-water preservationist movement to kill off some of the East's best fishing for rainbows and browns in a misguided attempt to restore Appalachian brook trout to lower-elevation waters, where they would provide at best marginal fishing.

But Steve says that isn't in the plans. "We'll restore only those areas we can realistically protect. Although they're not natives, rainbows and browns have a place here, too, especially in the lower elevations. But restoration is important for this park. Brook trout are our only natives. When you hike in to a place like the head of Deep Creek, with its virgin timber—oaks and hemlocks seven feet through at the butt—and its original-strain brook trout, you're seeing North America as it was before we came. And that's important."

It's always a little weird, this being home but not home. Home is gone, along with my father and my mother. Only my brother and I and our two children remain of this particular branch of Fishing Master Phillip Babb's line, and I live far to the north in Maine and my son is in Oregon, while Walter lives southeast of the little town where we grew up, where my great-grandfather and grandfather built the Methodist church along with the scant business block and half the brick downtowns in East Tennessee. Walter moved down-river to a little town closer to the mountains, an easier, quicker drive than the long, long hour and a half it used to take Dad's decrepit old Plymouth to struggle up into those cool familiar hills.

In a gravitational sense, home is now Walter's cabin perched precariously on Riddle Hill above the Tellico River, because it houses the last few remnants of my familiar childhood sights and smells, artifacts taken from closed-up family homes and converted to camp use: creels I'd tried to fill with trout as a boy now leading new lives as wall decorations amid the taxidermic excesses of my brother's early-twenties-trophy-trout phase. The stool where I perched, watching my mother make the featherlight rolls and cakes and pies that won her local renown. My grandmother's old stove and refrigerator, always ready with old-timey treats like fried chicken and stack-cake and fried pies and leather-britches beans boiled with sidemeat. My mother's good dishes, once out only on holidays and bridge-club meetings and now nicked and scratched and littered with the remains of ramps and trout and the odds and ends of feathers and fur, fallout from Walter's incessant fly tying, a part-time profession he has pursued since the age of nine. He fills boxes for his display at Little River Outfitters in the Smokies with old-time mountain flies like Thunderheads, Yaller Hammers, Specks, Yellow Palmers, and Tellico Nymphs, the latter a fly that's been around since before the turn of the century but which practically no one ties correctly anymore, with pale yellow wool ribbed with peacock and a pheasant tail back; the modern peacock-back variation with the yellow floss body is a far cry from the original pattern as marketed by the old E. H. Peckinpaugh Company, which is probably why people don't much use Tellico Nymphs anymore.

We fish Rick Blackburn's variation: A fisher or dark mink tail, golden yellow fur dubbing, three peacock herls twisted with tying thread for ribbing, a back of lacquered turkey, and a dark ginger wet-fly hackle palmered through the thorax; weighted, on a 3X-long hook, it's a crackerjack imitation of the big stonefly nymphs that crowd Appalachian streams from Maine to Tennessee.

I look around the cabin and its thrill of familiarity and feel at home, but I know that soon I'll have to head north to my other home, back to family and garden and job and an endless to-do list that flows over my bed at night like the credits from *Star Wars*.

My last day finds Walter and me high up on Roughridge Creek, climbing the rutted, overgrown remnants of the steep winding road to the old Melton place. Like all the old mountain homesteads in the national forest, this one is just a memory; its stout hand-split oak floorboards now form the subfloor of Walter's cabin, and its neat stone walls and incongruous fields of daffodils rise from a maturing forest where a garden once grew and where children once played. Where I once played.

Above the Melton place the trail becomes tenuous, and Roughridge Creek shrinks and accelerates its climb up Rough Ridge on the Tennessee-North Carolina line. Here live the original, unrestored Appalachian brook trout, and the old-timers know it. We're hoping to get high enough to find some they've missed, hoping to press on farther than they were willing to go. We alternately crawl on hands and knees and swing from vines, looking for a pool sufficiently clear of blowdowns to get a line in. When we find one we are invariably rewarded by a swift strike, but the brookies here are tiny—four or five inches. Finally I take a wildly leaping eight-inch male, impossibly red, a miniature fire truck with ridiculously exaggerated fins, a perfect photograph were there enough light in this Stygian tunnel to ready a camera before he twists from my wet palm. It is an all-too-brief encounter with the original fish, the true native of the Appalachians.

I watch him dart back into his refuge, a twisted gnarl of tree roots topped with a clump of Vasey's trillium, its deep maroon blossoms a blinding counterpoint to his bright crimson flanks.

I've driven thirteen hundred miles, walked maybe a hundred and change over the course of a week—all to catch a handful of fingerlings and one eight-inch fish.

Some would say only a fool would come this far for fish this small.

I feel a lot of things as I inhale the rich mountain air, then lean down and drink deeply from the chill waters of Roughridge Creek, the fleeting scent of trout and of deep-rooted home rising from my hands.

I feel a lot of things, but I don't feel at all like a fool.

2

Blue-Collar Cane

True nostalgia is an ephemeral composition of disjointed memories . . . but American-style nostalgia is about as ephemeral as copyrighted déjà vu.

—FLORENCE KING,
Reflections in a Jaundiced Eye

As we never-gonna-grow-up baby boomers lose our race with biological inevitability, we submerge ourselves in the trappings of our youth, as though to preserve it like a fly in amber. That's why nostalgia is the hot marketing phenom du jour. Just watch TV: We're still Bewitched, Dreaming of Jeannie, Leaving It to Beaver. Songs to which we once danced naked in the mud now sell us life insurance. Soon we'll see Mick Jagger pimping for denture adhesives, a laxative commercial backed by "I Can't Get No Satisfaction," an adult diaper ad alluding to the Dark Side of the Moon.

Smart Shoppes fill their shelves with so-called antiques marketed to forty-somethings who bought them years ago with pocket-change allowances, or unwrapped them beneath Eisenhower-era Christmas trees and set them out for curbside pickup at the onset of their Clearasil years. Even McCarthyism is back in style.

And then there are automobiles, America's cultural icon. Across the country, wherever cool sea breezes blow or leaves lose their chlorophyll, scenic highways fill with conga lines of old MGs, VW Beetles, and chopped-and-channeled cruisemobiles, and behind their obsolete wheels sit middle-aged Americans, within whose slumping bodies throb the hearts and minds of horny little teenagers.

When I was of the age, the object of desire was the 1955 Chevrolet, with its snarling, high-revving V8 and sharply modern looks then so startling after years of plodding dreary dough-dishes. Perhaps more than any other token of the era, a good '55 conjures memories of more innocent times: frenetic pep rallies, fumbling first dates, drive-in restaurants, drive-in movies, clandestine drag races, poodle-skirt spelunking in off-road passion pits.

Which is why nominally sane middle-aged men think nothing of spending upward of fifteen thousand dollars for a thirty-five-year-old car that handles like a tank and has only an AM radio. Denial is not just a river in Egypt, and if we can deny the passage of time with inanimate objects—or at least convince ourselves that we can—well, what the hell?

So it's no wonder that an aging fly-fishing obsessive who learned to cast with a nine-foot Montague while wearing a coon-skin hat and singing Born on a Mountaintop in Tennessee finds himself entering soft middle age with dreams of cane fly rods flexing through his head. I don't mean those frighteningly expensive works of art from Messrs. Gillum and Garrison, but the comparatively affordable blue-collar cane from Horrocks-Ibbotson. Montague. South Bend. Phillipson. Heddon. Granger. When I pick up one of those workingman's rods I am transported instantly back to halcyon days on the stream and long evenings around the campfire, listening to the grown-ups talk about fish and rods and life.

There's more than just nostalgia at work here. I own a number of top-end graphite rods and fish them whenever they're the most appropriate choice: tossing big streamers on long lines in icy spring gales; plopping big dry flies into heavy pocket water; drifting daisy chains of weighted nymphs and a fat indicator through deep secret runs; doing anything that involves salt water or travel in an airplane. But fishing graphite makes me hyperactive, as though I had just chased down a Halloween bag of Miniature Mounds with a quart of espresso. I come home from a day on the stream wired, crazed, out of breath. With my old cane rods I fish differently: slower, languid, almost dreamlike. I come home relaxed and at peace.

Not to put too anthropomorphic a twist on this, but a cane rod feels alive, like the stalk of giant grass from which it is split. And cane rods glow with a quiet inner warmth that comes only from organic materials shaped by the hands of artisans. Compared with my favorite old Heddon, a cheap rod in its day and not terrifically expensive now, most of my five-hundred-dollar graphite rods—hyperefficient marvels of space-age engineering though they may be—are as sterile and uninviting as a speculum.

You can thank (depending on whether you're aflame with the religious fervor of a recent cane convert) or blame (depending on whether you're scanning the used-rod lists for a good eight-footer for less than five hundred bucks) another famous baby boomer for the modern renaissance in cane fly rods. In his many books, John

Gierach writes often and convincingly of the tangible and intangible advantages of fishing cane, and in fact even devoted an entire book—*Fishing Bamboo*—to the subject.

I have John's books to thank and/or blame for my own conversion, or perhaps more accurately reconversion to cane a decade or so back, when I found myself fishing more and enjoying it less and wondering exactly what was missing. Turns out what was missing, at least for me, was a deep-remembered cadence and a totem— "the powerful mystique," as Gierach put it in his first book, *Fly Fishing Small Streams,* of fishing bamboo.

Like my father, I abandoned bamboo for fiberglass shortly after casting the wonder of its day: the Shakespeare Wonderod. That lithe little seven-footer bought on time with paper-route earnings from Wilburn's Hardware cast a pair of wet flies far more easily than did my creaking old nine-foot Montague, and it didn't need careful nightly drying or monthly waxing or annual revarnishing; you could lean it against a tree overnight without its morphing into a parabola; you could cast it all day without your rod hand turning to lead. And it was by-God modern.

That it was also a plug-ugly white noodle mattered little in the era's mad drive for modernity. Jets painted contrails from horizon to horizon. Cars sprouted fins. Little round monochromatic televisions became big and rectangular and spewed living color. A bleeping satellite named Telstar chased one called Sputnik across the night sky.

Who cared about the authentic past in those synthetic times? Who cared that those nightly fireside rituals of cane-rod maintenance were communal busywork that oiled conversation in a way merely staring into the fire did not?

Some folks cared. As we propped our plastic rods against trees and idled aimlessly around the fire, we laughed at the holdouts in our crowd, wasting their time drying and hanging and inspecting and puttering with those old-fashioned sticks. That they talked of good times gone by and we talked of days yet to come hardly seemed significant. We were modern. We didn't care. Even when they began fishing by themselves.

Many years later, or so it seemed—though when I do the math I realize my back-to-back experiments with the navy and urban life totaled only a half-dozen years, an eon in those days, an eyeblink now—a search for something real led me to Maine, looking for a chance to realign my front end with trees and fields and wild rivers. And to do justice to those wild rivers I needed a new fly rod.

I went to Dakin's Sporting Goods, an old-time Bangor institution where in the 1930s the Brady Gang's fumbling attempt to buy tommy guns in what they assumed was a dumb hick town ended in a spectacular shoot-out with G-men, where central Maine sports had bought rods and reels and shotguns for years, where the shiny and new mingled seamlessly with the dusty and old. I flexed and I wiggled and I sighted down shafts, and I came away owning a seven-foot Fenwick Ferralite. It was the latest thing, the hottest rod of its day—and it was only five dollars more than the seven-foot F. E. Thomas Dirigo that sat beside it on the shelf and in test-casting on Market Square came alive in my hand like a thing possessed. But it was dusty and old-fashioned and I was still agog with shiny and high-tech. I try not to remember, when I look at the scabrous old Fenwick leaning unloved in the back of the rod closet, that the forty-dollar Thomas is now worth something like twelve hundred bucks. Or that Dirigo, the Maine state motto, means "I Serve." I don't know what Ferralite means.

My brother and others like him weren't fooled. When the rest of us bought into the future they looked solidly to the past. When the rest of us were selling for peanuts our old Heddons and Edwardses and Grangers, even our Garrisons and Dickersons and Paynes and Youngs, they were snapping them up left and right. When the rest of us were moving into graphite and obsessing about line speed, my brother was fishing a seven-and-a-half-foot Orvis Battenkill so persistently that it gradually slid down the line-weight scale from five to one.

When I began looking for affordable cane about ten years ago, I got catalogs from the numerous dealers specializing in preowned fly tackle and was impressed with the wide selection and detailed descriptions. Anyone wanting to dip a toe in the old-cane waters can call folks like Martin Keane, Carmine Lisella, or Bob Corsetti and find just about anything imaginable. But there's no sport in it, no thrill of the hunt, no chance of finding a screeching bargain— and at the particular stage in my life when cane-lust resurfaced, little chance of finding a rod I really wanted for a price I could afford to pay. So I did what all Mainers of modest means do when the need arises for an affordable edition of anything from a fly rod to a size 16 wedding dress, "guaranteed never worn": I bought a copy of *Uncle Henry's,* a swap-and-sell magazine that is more than a Maine institution; it's the cornerstone of the blue-collar economy.

Most ads for "valuble antique bamboo flie rods" turned out to be uncastable Japanese knockoffs or bottom-end Montagues with split ferrules and delaminated sections. But one ad sounded promising, mentioning solid blue-collar names like Granger and even an Orvis. I dialed the number and got the seller's friend, who knew nothing about cane rods himself but assured me his buddy, who didn't have a phone, "had a whole trailer full of 'em. He don't like them graphite jobbies a-tall, but he just loves them old bamboo fly poles." I made a date to see them the next day.

The directions led me through one of those dreary dying mill towns notched into Maine's western foothills and into a chain of increasingly dilapidated roads, until I finally came to what my notes described as the third dirt road after the burned-out gas station sixteen miles from town, the first trailer on the right.

Two longhaired bearded men in flannel shirts and oil-stained jeans hovered over a 1950s-era Gale Buccaneer exhausting itself in a water-filled barrel marked DANGER—TOXIC. They were the kids who could fix cars in high school but could not conjugate verbs or even see the reason for trying, now grown up and left behind by an economy with no place for people good with their hands but not at following instructions. An old trailer disgorged a swarm of scruffy children into a bare yard filled with discarded auto parts and broken toys, and the smell of gear oil and beer hung like a cloud in the damp April air. I fought back a sneer of class-consciousness, an unfortunate legacy from my plantation-bred Maryland mother—something I hate in other people and positively despise in myself, having met far too many upper-crust pinheads and trailer-trash saints.

The rods were up at Dave's trailer. "It's up the rud a bit; hope you don't mind walkin'," he said, smearing outboard oil on his pants before shaking hands. The kids piled into the back of his rusted-out Toyota and bounced happily along with a tangle of smelt nets, gas cans, and chain saws as I followed Dave around hairpin turns and across washed-out culverts on a two-track spiraling up into a landscape just emerging from the dull wet slosh of early spring.

We stopped next to a pair of pallets lying across a flooded ditch and headed up a steep narrow trail that wound through cutover woodlands overlooking the broad valley of the Androscoggin. At trail's end sat a sagging trailer propped precariously on chunks of cordwood. "Dragged it up here over the snow with the skidder," Dave said, sweeping his arm proudly back at the vista. "Got me 160 acres of woods up here."

A big chocolate Lab snarled at the end of a short chain shackled to a rusted-out school bus filled with auto parts; bits of snow machines and a disassembled skidder littered the yard; a bowl of fresh smelt heads on a wobbly pallet porch drew mangy cats and buzzing flies and anxious anorexic chickens. A hawk circled lazily overhead, and the boys ran inside for an old Red Ryder BB gun and began firing at it.

Inside, the trailer stank of kerosene and mildew and past-due laundry. "'Scuse the mess. Wife run off down to Portland last year. Lemme light one these lanterns. Ain't got 'lectricity up here yet."

The soft lantern light revealed a museum of sporting goods: deer- and bearskins covered the furniture; deer heads, moose antlers, and large mounted fish covered the walls. Battered felt hats with flies stuck in the brims hanging from spikes; stacks of rod cases and bamboo rod parts stood in the corners; piles of old fly reels and fly boxes and lures covered tables; ancient greenheart and lancewood fly rods and double-barrel shotguns with Damascus-twist barrels and exposed hammers lay across deer-foot gun racks; a display case knocked together from pallet scraps held silk fly lines in their original boxes, gut leaders in silver soaking trays, a nickel-silver collapsible drinking cup marked ABERCROMBIE & FITCH, a minuscule Abbey & Imbrie casting reel, a Heddon Woodpecker plug in its original box, a boxful of tiny Heddon fly-rod plugs, a Carlton Ideal fly reel with a new silk line, a minnow made from white leather with a silver submarinelike diving plane in its original Kingfisher package, a jumble of perfect Maine streamers stuck on cards autographed with names like Herb Welch and Carrie Stevens. It was the combined wealth of a hundred years of Maine sporting tradition collected from countless garage sales.

"I hate to sell these rods, but I gotta get parts for the skidder and get it back workin' 'fore mud season's over. This here's the best of 'em," holding out a pedestrian eight-foot Orvis six-weight built indifferently from a kit. When I didn't appear interested he said, "It's a two-piece; I don't care for them three-piece rods much, but I got a bunch if you wanna see 'em," dragging from the bedroom an armload of aluminum tubes.

I looked through them quickly: half a dozen ho-hum Montagues, an old Chubb some ten feet long, a Bangor Leonard salmon rod, a well-used Bristol F-12, an ancient rod with hand-turned ferrules, tunnel guides, full red intermediate wraps, and a silver reel seat signed Jay Harvey.

I was after usable trout rods, not collectibles, so I selected a nine-foot five-weight Goodwin Granger Victory, an eight-foot six-weight Sewell Dunton Anglers' Choice with a fancy walnut seat and Super-Z ferrules, a high-end nine-foot Montague Red Wing from the 1930s that seemed unused, the scent of tung-oil varnish rushing from the opened tube like ghosts from a mummy's tomb.

"How much for these three?"

He named a figure that sounded high to me, and I set them aside.

He kept bringing out rods, reels, flies—as anxious as a ten-year-old to show off his collection, to have me admire his stuff, to see what he'd picked up over the years. The idea of parting with any of it clearly saddened him, but old fly tackle doesn't put meals on the table. A working skidder, in this corner of Maine where self-employed logging is about the only job left for the nonconjugators of verbs, the nonmanipulators of data or peddlers of real estate, that's what puts meals on the table.

"Ya wanna cast them rods?"

We walked out into the dooryard, rigged up the Granger and the Dunton and the Montague, and began casting and talking. He had the easy fluid stroke of a natural and sent perfect candy-cane loops sailing across the field.

"My dad and I fished together 'bout every day when I was a kid. He always fished cane, never liked them plastic rods. Said they didn't have no soul. Said cane was good enough for his dad and it was good enough for him. These rods here," he said, picking up fifty feet of line and sending it sailing out with a flick of the wrist, "they got a life to 'em. When I cast these rods I feel somehow like I'm still fishin' with my dad."

"I know what you mean," I said. "You two still fish together?"

"Nope. He got killed at the mill when I was twelve. You?"

"Smoked himself to death about ten years ago."

We continued casting for a while, saying nothing. As the sun began to sink into the hills I finally cased the three rods, wrote him a check for his asking price, shook his hand, wished him luck, and drove slowly back down to the coast, finally shutting off the windshield wipers when I realized it wasn't evening fog blurring my vision.

3

Fishing with a Wet Fly

And as you sit on the hillside, or lie prone under the trees of the forest, or sprawl wet-legged on the shingly beach of a mountain stream, the great door, that does not look like a door, opens.

—STEPHEN GRAHAM,
The Gentle Art of Tramping

I hate waders. Few things more efficiently leach the carefree contentment from fly fishing. They are a frail and solemn responsibility, like a new Easter suit or an ancient maiden aunt.

Have you ever left unfished a perfect pool because the only possible path to the one good casting spot led through a wild tangle of briers and barbed wire—and you were wearing new waders? Yeah. Me too.

Wader technology has come a long way since the days of board-stiff rubberized canvas. We've progressed through all-rubber, latex, coated nylon, neoprene, and more recently breathable waders made with Gore-Tex and its imitators. Each was an incremental improvement over its predecessor, ever lighter, ever more comfortable, but each suffers from the same drawbacks: High-tech to low, waders are fragile and confining, a numbing barrier between ourselves and that magical marriage of hydrogen and oxygen where anglers go to play.

To me, few experiences match the sensual pleasures of standing thigh-deep in cold, swift-flowing water. Distanced from the current only by the thin fabric of lightweight trousers, I feel what those great canoe men, the French-Canadian voyageurs, called *la fil d'eau,* the thread of the water—rhythmic variations in hydraulic pressure: water music, to put a Handel on it. In wild rapids it thrums against my legs like Wagnerian low brass; in majestic pools it becomes ponderously Purcellian; in endless pocket water it is a rollicking version of the Grateful Dead's "Ripple"—a tangible musical thread connecting me to the world of trout in ways I cannot explain. In waders, the beat comes through muffled and dull, like one of those wheeled woofers Dopplering the bass clef of music you're glad you don't recognize. I stumble and slide, an echo-ranging bat wearing earmuffs.

I used to dismiss all this as a load of revenant Aquarian Age claptrap, something subliminally rekindled by a stray copy of *Utne Reader.* Then, after an evening of journalistic investigations into the microbrewery phenomenon with a couple of other fish-writers, I confessed that I often wondered whether I fly fished only because it provides a plausible excuse to stand all day in running water. I was startled to see furtive flickers of recognition.

Many of us, it appears, enjoy spending the day with wet pants. This is a guilty pleasure available only to anglers, for under the cover of a fishing rod we become harmless bumblers licensed to perform acts in public that in others would be considered suspect, even alarming.

In frigid areas like New England and the Pacific Northwest, and in most trout-fishing areas early and late in the season, waders are a necessary evil. Hypothermia is even less fun than smearing snail trails of Aquaseal over shredded neoprene, and long-term immersion in cold water can lead to circulatory problems that may redefine angling in your sunset years as dangling something limp from a boat. But even when fishing small streams in warm climates, many of today's anglers don chest waders as routinely as they fit reels to rods. I can't remember the last time I saw a beaming angler in a fly-fishing magazine who wasn't bewadered to the collarbone—even in ankle-deep water in midsummer Montana.

Growing up in the East Tennessee hills, you miss out on a lot of trends. I was eighteen and in the navy before I saw my first pizza, or knew that the cheese sprinkled on spaghetti wasn't pronounced parMEEzeyun or a paper bag wasn't a poke. I was in my twenties and freshly moved to Maine before I first saw an angler wearing chest waders. When I stepped into the Penobscot wearing only chinos on that warm May day and my tears froze, I found out why.

Things were so much easier when I was a kid. When we weren't in school or at church, boys had only one acceptable uniform: pegleg bluejeans and a white T-shirt—the James Dean look. We fished in a worn-out pair of high-top P. F. Flyers with indoor-outdoor carpeting glued to the soles, two pairs of wool socks, and a pair of blue jeans. Trouble is, once wet, blue jeans never truly dry, and they become colder and heavier as the day wears on.

And white T-shirts? My father graphically demonstrated what they do to your fish-catching potential by walking slowly up to a tailout on crystal-clear Doublecamp Creek, where a big pair of fat browns hung sipping nymphs. He was wearing his old World War II-pattern camouflage shirt, and the browns didn't move a muscle. Then he invited his pair of miniature James Deans to join him. We moved in like Indians ghosting through the woods, and the browns vanished like smoke.

I can't figure out whether this wader dependency of today's anglers stems from fashion-consciousness or from a subliminal squirming away from actual contact with the wild by city folks whose parents said one too many times, "Don't touch that; you don't know where it's been."

Waders are a literal as well as a figurative burden. I prefer to fish waters where hordes of well-read scientific anglers have not yet made the trout smarter than me. Fortunately, even in these over-crowded days a walk of only a few miles can transport you to near-virgin territory. But a long walk in waders—or their low-water equivalent, hip boots—is less a pleasant stroll through the woods than an interminable trudge, a trail of tears through a gauntlet of malevolence.

Of course you can always carry your waders. You might as well carry your wading shoes, too, because although felt soles are reasonably slip-proof on wet rocks, on dry pine needles and forest duff they are lethal. I have fallen several orders of magnitude more often en route to a stream than in the stream itself. A hike in felt-sole shoes is a trudge liberally laced with stumbles and the occasional screaming fall. No wonder today's anglers fish ever closer to the parking lot.

But carrying waders and wading shoes adds another five to ten pounds to the already considerable burden of the well-equipped modern fly fisher. And when you arrive huffing and puffing at your destination and change into your waders, you must then lug around a bulky pair of back-thunking four-pound hiking shoes all day, unless you're better at finding cached equipment than I am. I'm still looking for a fine pair of Fabianos I hid near the mouth of Webster Stream some twenty years back. Perhaps they became part of an unsolved mystery. "We found shoes," I see a conscientious vacationing urbanite telling a warden as she holds them up and shakes them at his face, "but no body."

We need this freedom from extraneous burdens as we age and begin to lose our lifelong battle with gravity. We also need, above all else, nonslip soles. But with the exception of carbide-studded shoes—tenacious on ice or thick moss but a clacking, skidding abomination practically everywhere else—fly-fishing footwear technology has until very recently remained static.

L. L. Bean, the outdoor institution founded on the sole of a pair of brilliant ideas—mating waterproof rubber bottoms with breathable leather tops and throwing in an unconditional lifetime guarantee of "100% satisfaction in every way"—has its Aqua Stealth wading shoes, conventional Abner Yokumesque brogans mated with knobby black soles molded of a sticky rubber compound burgled from the rock-climbing footwear industry. Chota, an East Tennessee company, has its Brookies—running-shoe clones with ripple-rubber soles having inset felt pads at ball and heel. And Weinbrenner, maker of the ubiquitous Gary Borger Ultimates, is toying with a gummy new sole from Vibram that I haven't tried yet but which looks promising.

All offer advantages over felt on the trail in to the stream, but so far none approaches the sheer stickiness of old-fashioned wool felt once you get there, though both the Bean and Chota offerings get pretty close to the tractive tenacity of hard-woven polyester felt. They're compromises, and like all compromises they're not particularly satisfying solutions to the problem at hand, but at least they're better than the alternatives of lugging extra shoes or falling on your ass trying to navigate a steep trail in to the stream.

Of course once you get to the stream, you've still got to decide whether you want to fish dry and warm but distanced from the fish's world or trade the immediacy of becoming one with the fish for a possible future of becoming one with a walker.

There are technological work-arounds here, too, in the guise of fast-drying nylon pants and waterproof, breathable knee socks, DuPont SealSkinz being one brand that's worked well for me. Compared with waders, even the waist-high breathables that have become my virtual uniform, these things are as surgical gloves are to oven mitts.

The combination is also perfect for the amphibious style of fishing common to the North Country, where you are in and out of the canoe dozens of times a day, wading to fish a riffle or portaging around beaver dams and riverine blockages of white-water rafters collectively inventing wild tales with which to bore their coworkers around urban-office watercoolers.

Too many artificial barriers separate us from our environment these days—air conditioning, Muzak, and e-mail come to mind. At least in angling we can enjoy the occasional freedom of dipping into the fish's world unencumbered by a pair of thick rubber britches.

So try this: Some nice summer day, leave your waders in the car and go light, the way most of us did when fly fishing was still just a sport and not yet an industry. Wade wet, feel for the thread of the water, and perhaps a door will open.

4

The Indicator Papers

*Nothing so needs reforming as other people's
habits.*—MARK TWAIN, *Pudd'nhead Wilson*

*I*f you enjoy human conflict as spectator sport, but boxing
has grown stale since ear biting became socially unaccept-
able and professional wrestling seems merely a trailer-park pro-
duction of *Faust,* here's a suggestion: Find a gathering of serious
fly fishers—Trout Unlimited or FFF meetings are good spots, but
a busy fly shop will do in a pinch as will, for the digitally inclined,
a fly-fishing newsgroup like the continually contentious Rec.out-
doors.fishing.fly—and take a strong stand on strike indicators. It
doesn't matter whether you're for or against them; either way
you'll have all the fighting you care to see.

The strike-indicator faction likes them because in certain situations they make fly fishing easier. The vociferous minority of

anti-indicatorites despises them for exactly the same reason. Anything that makes fly fishing easier, goes the argument, saps the sport of its essence and flouts its time-honored traditions. I suppose a fly fisher using an eighteen-foot ash rod with a plaited horsehair line and a Berners-model fly tied on a hook hand-forged from a sewing needle has a right to peer down on the unenlightened from an historically superior pedestal, but for someone using a thin tube of aerospace-derived graphite composite to propel a microbubble-impregnated plastic line and extruded nylon leader tipped with an entomologically perfect imitation of a hatch-chart-identified dun toward a trout spotted with eyeglasses designed to restrict the passage of light vibrating in other than a single plane and thereby eliminate the surface glare that has shielded fish from predators for eons, that lofty perch starts to wobble.

Strike indicators are tools, like duct tape, cordless drills, or guns—inanimate objects, neither good nor evil. Although kidnappers bind victims with duct tape, and cordless drills and guns aid and abet all sorts of mayhem, only product-liability lawyers and the voluntarily illogical believe those tools acted of their own volition.

So it's natural to assume that fly fishing's inquisition du jour is targeted less toward innocuous bits of plastic and yarn that help track the movements of subsurface flies than toward the people who use them.

I blame the British. In his 1857 book, *The Practical Angler*, W. C. Stewart wrote that you could catch more fish more easily by fishing upstream. A decade or so later, Frederick Halford began writing that in certain circumstances you could catch more fish more easily using dry flies. It didn't take long for their apostles to go from *Here are two really effective ways to catch trout*, to *Here is the only way a gentleman catches trout: upstream and on the dry.*

Even today, some folks feel dry-fly fishing is celestially anointed, and nymphing and other unsavory habits rank just above tossing niblet corn with a Pocket Fisherman.

I'll enthusiastically agree that few public acts are more thrilling than the sight of a trout snorting your elegant little dun from the surface. But if the trout aren't looking up—and they usually aren't, biologists and experience tell us—then dry-fly fishing becomes only an aesthetically pleasing form of self-abuse.

And there's a logical flaw in the dry fly's canonization: Compared with nymph fishing, dry-fly fishing is easy. A dry fly is always visible and the strike unmistakable; even the terminally clueless know when to set the hook. But a nymph is submerged and therefore invisible, and the trout's underwater take is subtle and fleeting.

Nymph specialists develop an almost-supernatural ability to detect strikes. Their eyes never leave their line, and their line is always slightly under tension, traveling at precisely current speed and ready to telegraph even the most minute drift anomaly that signals *strike*. Combine those finely honed predatory senses with the biological truth that trout eat more submerged nymphs than floating imagoes, and it's no wonder that pioneering American nymphmeister Edward Hewitt claimed a nymph fisher who knows what he's about can clean out a stream.

Fortunately, that's not entirely accurate, for tight-line nymphing is a short-range game. At distances beyond, say, thirty feet, that telepathic connection with the fly so important to sensing a strike withers away; worse, the nymph becomes ever more subject to the baleful influence of drag, both from the vagaries of current and the catenary of line. Of course minimizing drag is crucial to dry-fly fishing, too, but velocity changes on a two-dimensional surface are plainly visible and an avoidance path more or less readily plotted. With nymphs, drag is three-dimensional and largely invisible.

And this is where the strike indicator becomes valuable as more than a mere indicator of strikes, for a nymph suspended from an indicator can be positioned accurately in the water column; it is free to follow current whims and virtually free from drag, especially if the indicator is deftly mended upstream of the nymph; it can be fished as far off as you can cast and still see your indicator. Better yet (or what's worse, depending on your personal piety), minute up-and-down variations in the water's surface animate a suspended nymph in a convincingly realistic fashion. Of course in the view of traditional dogmatists, it's this self-guiding, self-animating ability that makes catching trout with an indicator-and-nymph too easy and thus invites their scorn—this despite some four hundred years of fly-fishing literature uniformly dedicated to making it easier to catch trout. At least I can't remember any innovations specifically intended to make it harder to catch trout.

Strike indicators as such may be comparatively new, but aiding strike detection and easing drag management by suspending a nymph or wet fly from a floating device certainly isn't. In the southern Appalachians, and presumably most everywhere else, folks were using dry flies as strike indicators at least as far back as the 1920s. When I started fly fishing in the 1950s almost everyone I knew fished that way. I still do, as often as not, and I never recall being branded an heretic for doing so, either, although I will admit that I've tried to follow my mother's warning to be careful of the company I keep. Perhaps someone fishing an indicator dry receives special dispensation, as you're just as likely to catch fish on it as on the tagalong nymph. Or perhaps roving inquisitors just see your dry and assume you're an initiate. Besides, where I grew up in East Tennessee, a purist who commented unfavorably on an unknown angler's choice of fly-fishing disciplines would be either recklessly ignorant or suicidal.

I've tried many different dry flies as indicators; none was superior and all sank sooner or later, especially with something big and ugly and weighted at tippet's end. A Humpy is the default-choice indicator, and some folks swear by a heavily hackled Elk Hair Caddis, often with a clipped deer hair body. A simple Devil Bug works as well as anything, and I keep thinking that someday I ought to try one with an unsinkable underbody of closed-cell foam instead of tying thread, although that may be verging into heresy of the synthetic-versus-natural-materials vein.

There are various schools of thought on attaching an indicator dry. The time-honored method is turle-knotting the dry fly to the tippet knot's tag end so it cantilevers an inch or so off the leader. This gives you a good drift, but it's hard to cast and spends too much time devising Gordian knots to tax your eyesight and patience, especially if you forget about the nymph and start false-casting to pop water off the dry.

Some folks simply thread the dry fly onto the leader before tying on the tippet, so that it slides back against the tippet knot, and others tie both the leader and the tippet to the dry fly's eye. These are both easy to rig, and compared with a dry fly on a dropper they are easier to cast and almost tangle-free, but I've never been able to get a decent drift out of the dry fly; it tends to cock at an angle to the current and scoot around on the surface like a water-skier cutting wakes. It's fun to watch and often annoys Atlantic salmon into striking, but trout don't seem all that interested.

Out West they like to tie the nymph and tippet directly to the dry fly's bend. This is definitely the easiest two-fly rig to cast, it seldom tangles, and because the two flies are precisely in line it gives the best drift of any method I've tried, especially if the dry fly has some extra flotation aft—a Humpy with an extra-fat moose hair tail, for instance. I suspect you miss some fish that come after the dry fly from astern and sheer off after running afoul of the dangling tippet, but I can't really prove it.

Every year a new crop of strike indicators comes to market, but all fall into just a few categories: Yarn, pinch-on foam, slide-on plastic or cork, and the one I prefer, a moldable starch-based plastic goo that looks like those orange marshmallow peanuts folks who don't like children give to trick-or-treaters on Halloween.

Loon Outdoors seems to have originated this stuff, although it's available in tubs imprinted with a variety of brand names. The beauty of it is, you can pinch off just what you need and form it into an aerodynamic shape that's fairly easy to cast, and you can strip it off your line quickly and stuff it back in the container if you decide to change tactics or care that a nearby purist is glaring at you like you're passing gas in holy water. It's also claimed to be biodegradable—an important consideration, since in my informal surveys, cast-off strike indicators comprise the second most common bankside litter in fly-fishing-only areas, right after expensive cigar butts.

When fishing a nymph at close range I often hit a leader knot or two with a tiny pinch of this goo—just enough to make things easier for my sad eyesight and sorry attention span. If I'm fishing a little farther out and want to suspend a nymph, I'll roll a bigger gob around the leader into a cigar shape. Beyond shelled-cashew size, however, it becomes too heavy to cast gracefully and plops on the water like a bass bug.

Then it's time for a hunk-o-yarn. You can buy this nicely put up in official fly-fishing packages for a couple of bucks per foot, or you can go to a sewing or craft store and get a lifetime supply for a quarter. Wool yarn works okay if well greased, but it's better to find something lighter than water, like polyethylene or polypropylene.

The conventional way of fishing a yarn indicator is just knotting it to your leader as far above your fly as you want it to float, but a far better system, also from Out West, is a right-angle outrigger. Tie your leader (a clinch knot works fine) to the middle of a two-inch or so hank of yarn, then tie your tippet and fly to the leader in front of the yarn. It's hard to imagine a system harder to cast, but it suspends a nymph beautifully and is virtually free from catenary pull, since the fly dangles straight down from the bobber, er uh, indicator.

I watched a twelve-year-old kid fishing one of these rigs in a Hallowed Pool on the West Branch of the Penobscot last year. His hunk of neon green yarn was so big I thought at first he was fishing with a dead parakeet. He had a lot of other strikes against him, too: His equipment was cheap and brand new, he was an unstylish caster, and he was wearing a cowboy hat with a feather in it. The other fishermen in the pool watched him with that mixture of grudging forbearance and thinly veiled disgust that has somehow become the proper way to welcome newcomers to the gentle sport of fly fishing.

And, of course, the kid had the poor judgment to catch three nice salmon while nearby anglers with far more experience and infinitely better taste in both equipment and headgear went fishless. The general atmosphere around the pool did cheer considerably when he lost a two-footer as fat as a Florida bass, but he may have sensed the surrounding moral outrage and tangled his dimestore net with his cowboy hat on purpose.

While we're shoveling out blame for the denominational schisms in fly fishing, let's save some for the trout themselves, for it's not just the strike indicator's ability to help marginal fly fishers catch outsize fish that maddens the anti-indicatorites, but that salmonids—those X-ray-vision ultra-entomologists that we all know spurn flies imperfect in size, shape, or hue—often strike the indicators themselves. And sometimes damned hard. So hard that, at one time or another, every angler who ever fished an indicator has at least thought about pinching a tab of fluorescent foam around a bare hook and tossing it out.

Of course if any caught a fish, not even Torquemada could extract a confession.

5

The Great Bream Expeditions

The desire to make off with the substance of others is the foremost—the most legitimate— passion nature has bred into us . . . and, without doubt, the most agreeable one.

—MARQUIS DE SADE,
Juliette; ou, Les Prospérités du Vice

*W*e are a nation with public personae and private passions: celebrated social commentators obsessed with Beavis and Butthead; prominent gourmands gobbling burgers and fries; pompadoured televangelists furtively Websurfing for anatomical improbabilities dot com. We visit one therapist to liberate our inner child and another to bottle him up again. We join twelve-step programs that replace one addiction with another, and we appear on Sally Jessy Whatserface to broadcast urges we hide from our neighbors.

Why should I be different? I live in the heart of trout and salmon country and have a public love affair with the salmonids in general and brook trout in particular, and I have been lucky enough for this to become, as Trollope's Reverend Septimus Harding would say, "a living."

But I too have a secret craving—a fish found not in aristocratic trout streams but in pedestrian ponds and murky impoundments; a fish with the power to transmogrify a sophisticated, law-abiding sportsman into a larcenous scofflaw.

Hello. My name is Jim and I have a thing for bream.

Bream, Brim, Sun Perch, Sunnies, Bluegills, Shellcrackers, Redears, Longears. Call them what you will, the various members of the Centrarchid family are the most universal piscine quarry in the lower forty-eight and ideal fish for fly rodders: ubiquitous and insectivorous, hard fighting and sweet fleshed, with a reproductive profligacy that makes catching them a near-certainty and eating them a guiltless pleasure. Curiously, many "serious" anglers ignore this wide-flung resource, relegating bream—and here I'm using my East Tennessee vernacular to describe any member of the sunfish family not known generically and incorrectly as bass—to the lumpen category of panfish, fit only for freckle-faced inhabitants of Norman Rockwell paintings and snuff-dipping old ladies wearing sun-visored straw hats and wrinkled Supp-hose.

Real anglers fish for bream, goes conventional wisdom, only to hone their skills for the more challenging business of fishing for trout. But trout are rather primitive fish (embryonic scales, no thorny protective spines) with simple brains and simple needs. In the classic trout environment, survivors of childhood brushes with cannibalism face few dangers beyond the odd osprey, otter, heron, or the comparatively recent threat from rod-waving representatives of *H. sapiens.*

For bream of any size, however, life has long been far more dangerous, and only the most wary and intelligent survive the constant onslaughts of binge-feeding bass, tooth-chopping gar, and hogmouth catfish, not to mention, in the Deep South, bowfin, alligators, and snapping turtles. Except for the vaguely unsporting practice of yanking them off their spawning beds, when they are far less likely to attack a fly because your angling artistry has convinced them it's food than because they are biologically compelled to protect their nests from invaders, big bream, especially bluegills, are harder to fool with an artificial fly than a six-pound springcreek brown.

We learned this as children, my brother and I. We were raised to be God-fearing trout fishermen and taught by a master, but the nearest trout was an hour and half's drive, and good bream fishing was less than a half hour's walk down the Southern Railway main line. We went after bream in Fort Loudoun Lake almost every day—sometimes together, sometimes alone. And we got pretty good at it, too. A boyhood friend recently told me that the thing he best remembered about the old days was the sight of one or both Babb Boys trudging down the railroad tracks trailing a huge stringer of bream. "Those were probably the biggest brim I've seen to this day," Tom said. "You boys was sure good fishermen."

We were indeed, for we had learned to read the signs.

For experienced bream fishermen, stump fields, weed beds, and overhanging trees sporting wasp nests or catalpa worms are surefire pointers to good fishing. But in a quest for ever bigger bream in a heavily fished lake, we found that the best signs of all said DANGER. KEEP OUT. NO TRESPASSING.

Our standard spot was the maintenance barge on the upstream side of the dam. We'd mingle with tourists and sightseers, walking slowly and innocently along the winding pedestrian path toward the visitor's center, unjointed fly rods held behind us and eyes riveted on the TVA offices crouched watchfully on the dam's shoulder. As we drew near and the coast looked clear, we'd slowly drop from sight, pressing against the dam's face and inching our way down to a narrow catwalk leading to the barge and its tool shed—and its sign reading NO TRESPASSING PER ORDER OF TENNESSEE VALLEY AUTHORITY.

Protected from officious eyes by the shed's overhanging roof and by a strategically placed bridge abutment, we'd lie on our bellies between the barge house and dam and watch thick schools of bream finning slowly along in the clear depths below. The trick was to lower a lightly weighted nymph through the school, letting the little ones take it and spit it out until one of the big boys edged slowly forward, inspecting the fly closely from all sides before finally darting in to inhale it. And you had to be damned quick on the trigger to set the hook before he spat it out. After the fight—and I know of no fish anywhere near its size with the unrelenting ferocity and sheer mechanical leverage of a big bluegill—we'd let the barge school settle down for a bit then try another fly.

Those were big bream by local standards; mostly bluegills and redbreasts and the occasional shellcracker, averaging a respectable five to six and occasionally seven inches. But for bream measured in pounds—the ultimate badge of a bream fisher's prowess—a riskier expedition was needed.

Halfway between the powerhouse offices on one side of the ninety-seven-foot-high dam and the lock control tower near the other were nine water-filled pools a little larger than a snooker table—backflows and maintenance access, I'm guessing, for the water inlets to the generating turbines far below. I first noticed them on a sixth-grade field trip, my fisherman's instincts alerted by a smell like old sardines. At first I saw only dark grimy water filled with floating trash and dead shad minnows, but as I continued to watch a pair of fat rubbery lips rose slowly and closed over a minnow, and suddenly I lost all interest in our droning tour guide's spiel about cheap electricity and freedom from devastating floods through the beneficence of the American taxpayer. Jeezus what a bream! And what a fishing hole! And what a threatening cluster of NO FISHING signs. And what a fine view the guards had from the TVA buildings a quarter mile off at either end of the dam.

But I hadn't invested all that time watching war movies to be defeated this easily, especially not in the Tennessee River Valley, susceptible as it is to frequent soupy fogs and monsoonal rainstorms. The next time a front passed through there'd be a *real* bream expedition. And I'd keep this spot to myself—no brother, no nobody. In the adolescent pecking order of the small-town South, those big bream would make me boss hawg.

And they were monsters: at least a foot long and some nearly that high; black as the Ace of Spades, with mean flaming eyes, dirty orange bibs, and humped foreheads like Saturday-matinee aliens. The first stringerload held a dozen fish averaging nearly two pounds, and more followed with each dip of the barometer.

I could have gotten away with it, too, if my father hadn't bragged around town about all the giant bream his boy was bringing home. "Biggest thangs I ever seen," he told his breakfast cronies at the Bus Station Restaurant. "But boys they're awful fishy tastin'." It didn't take long for a TVA guard—a distant cousin, like pretty near everyone else thereabouts—to venture a guess where those fish were coming from. "Doc," Bert said. "That there's a *FED*-rul crime." And it didn't take long for Dad to convince me I could find better ways to spend my time.

It didn't take long to find one, either. A friend had gotten wind of a hog farmer with a pond that had, he swore, some of the biggest bream ever seen in those parts. "He won't mind if we fish it," Sonny said, with an air of authority based entirely on the conviction that the hog farmer was headed to the Knoxville livestock auction for the day.

"How we gonna get there?" I whined. "It's better'n ten mile."

"No problem," Sonny said. "I got wheels."

"Do what?" I said. "You ain't no older'n twelve."

"Don't worry," he said. "I said I got wheels and I got wheels."

Next morning he pulled up to the house driving a big red Farmall M with vague statements of ownership; I hopped on the drawbar and we took off, following a circuitous and we hoped devious path through town before shifting into high and speeding down Martel Road. Finally we pulled into a little two-track through the kudzu, unslipped a gate, and chugged back under the pines to find the perfect bluegill pond, its water all lily pads and its banks all overhanging trees. Even as we jointed our rods we could see dimpled rises dotting its surface.

They were big, all right—not as big as the penstock bream, but big enough and far more brightly colored, and they were hungry. We'd have had a legendary day of fishing, too, if the pond's owner, a Poppin' Johnny Deere man drawn to the alien four-cylinder drone of a Farmall on his back forty, hadn't shown up accompanied by two very pissed-off parents, alerted, we later learned, by a new countywide spy network of busybody cousins intent on heading off any further incidents of hooliganism and who had tracked our progress all morning.

On the way home, facing a constant stream of Old Testament retribution and the very real possibility of military school banishment, even I became nervous about my budding life of crime, at the root of which finned an innocent and ubiquitous little fish beloved of freckle-faced kids and old ladies in straw hats.

⋆   ⋆   ⋆

I often say that I moved to Maine for the brook trout and Thoreau's wild North Woods and the joys of living in an inbred rural community where none of the cousins are mine, but I privately wonder if I was just trying to put temptation far behind me. In forty-some years of trout fishing I have never once fished in closed waters, never stretched a fish to make the length limit, never tipped a fly with bait in FFO waters. I have never hunted out of season, never exceeded a bag limit, never shot at ducks with the case of pre-prohibition high-base lead #4s moldering away in the shed. It is only bream that arouse my basest instincts, and here in Maine there simply aren't any, not really. Oh, there are sunfish—stunted pumpkinseeds and redbreasts and the incidental tiny bluegill—but they're so small and uninteresting that even children and old ladies ignore them. White perch *(Morone americana),* the locally favored panfish, are abundant, grow as large as two or three pounds, and are wonderfully tasty, but they are indifferent fighters and unlovely to behold, their monochromatic bodies resembling the carplike European bream *(Abramis brama)* whose name European colonists unfairly settled on the elegant and unrelated members of the sunfish tribe.

So I console myself with trout and salmon and only occasionally think about long-past bream expeditions, adolescent angling transgressions being less easily forgiven a middle-aged man and inexcusable in an outdoor writer. Besides, I'm guessing not many outdoor writers can get a living from writing about bream, not even by Septimus Harding's standards, although for reasons beyond my ken the salmonids seem to support an inordinate number of us.

Still, I could feel the old lawless urges stirring when I headed to Augusta, Georgia, a few years ago to meet my new colleagues at

Gray's Sporting Journal and maybe, said Ed-in-C Dave Foster and his fishing buddy Ben Estes, get in a little bass fishing on a network of private ponds, including one with the intriguing name of Cardiac.

"Uh, any bluegills around?" I'd asked. Oh sure, they'd said, plenty. But when Ben talked constantly about giant Florida large-mouths that looked like garbage cans with gills and suggested a nine-weight with a lot of backbone and popping bugs the size of ducklings, I sensed bluegills might be an incidental quarry.

As it turned out we caught the beejezus out of bass, so many that my lipping thumb swelled up like a turnip. And when Ben wasn't looking I snuck a tiny nymph onto a dropper off the bend of a popping bug and caught a couple of frightened-looking bream—the designated food fish in the stump-garden bass paradise that was Cardiac Pond. One pleasant evening at a different pond we even targeted bream specifically, catching enough nice bluegills and shellcrackers for a big fish fry at Ben's house on Clark's Hill Reservoir.

And while it was fun and all, I headed back for Maine feeling hollow and unsatisfied, as though I had gone to a pig pulling and eaten only coleslaw. It was, I think, the sight of all those NO TRESPASSING signs guarding the private water we fished; the long, winding, plantation-era drives protected by locked gates to which only the wealthy owners and their privileged guests had the keys.

Lacking the forbidden seasoning of larceny, bream seemed just another fish.

6

The Idiocy of Youth

*There is no man, however wise, who has not
at some period of his youth said things, or
lived in a way the consciousness of which is so
unpleasant to him in later life that he would
gladly, if he could, expunge it from his memory.*

—MARCEL PROUST,
Remembrance of Things Past

oday I fished Big White Brook—a thoroughly unremarkable
little mountain stream tucked into an out-of-the-way corner
of north-central Maine. Thanks to acid rain and strip-mine forestry
the fishing these days isn't what it used to be, but I'm here less for
today's fishing than for yesterday's, for this is the last place I fished
with my father. It was 1973, and he and my mother and aunt had
come north to reestablish lines of communication severed in the
generational strife of The Sixties. But we had never really commu-
nicated, my family and I. Unless the subject was fishing.

Norman Maclean wrote that in his family there was no clear line between religion and fly fishing, but in ours the line was sharply defined: On April 15 trout season opened, and the best church choir in East Tennessee lost its star bass singer and his two young understudies until the season ended in the fall. All winter long we sang that some day we'd cross over Jordan and dwell in Beulah Land, but come summer we found our own Beulah Land in the here and now of high-mountain streams and rivers.

I no more remember learning to fish than I remember learning to walk. We had always fished, my father and older brother and me. We lived in a little red-clay farm town at the juncture of the Tennessee and Little Tennessee Rivers, and Walter and I spent our days along their banks, looking for arrowheads and fishing for whatever we could find: bream, stripers, sauger, drum, catfish. In the evening Dad would take us to the lake, or to our cousin John Browder's farm on a remote loop of the Tennessee River for popping-bug bluegills and the occasional bass. Weekends and vacations we'd drive an hour and a half into the mountains for trout, camping in the old army wall tent alongside a favorite stream—North River, Bald River, Roughridge Creek, Sycamore Creek, Citico Creek—and gorging on trout in quantities now hard to believe and, viewed through the lens of catch-and-release presentism, impossible to justify.

We were dedicated fly fishermen in a land where most folks fished for trout with canned corn and a significant minority favored Clorox or dynamite, yet we never thought of ourselves as elite purists looking down on the hill-country hoi polloi, as did the fancy city boys from Knoxville and 'Lanta who sometimes wandered into these mountains with fly rods in hand, mistaking them for part of the government-civilized Smokies just to the north. We *were* the hoi polloi—just homespun hillbillies, perhaps

better read than most, who had inherited a more engaging, entertaining, and frequently more effective way of catching trout.

Those southeastern Tennessee mountains were rough places in
those days—copperheads, moonshiners, Russian hogs, more copperheads. In parts they're still rough places, especially now that the
moonshiners' kids have branched out, so to speak, into other
intoxicating enterprises grown in remote patches guarded with all
the savage ingenuity some two hundred years of isolation and a
couple of tours in Vietnam can devise. If you think James Dickey's
Deliverance was a wild flight of fancy, I'll turn you on to some great
fishing if you'll make me your sole beneficiary.

Dad used to tell of the time a drunken flatlander climbed the
Monroe County courthouse steps and hollered "I kin whup anybody in town." When the smoke cleared he had so many holes in
him that he fluttered soundlessly to the ground, like a leaf.

We never had any problems. Everybody thereabouts knew and
liked bass-singin' Babb. At his funeral, prim politicians crowded
onto church pews alongside noted town characters like Paddlefoot
Aikens and Lambseye Dailey, and massed church choirs from across
Loudon County sang tribute to a man with a wealth of friends and
no enemies.

Dad was an unlikely-looking likable guy. Razor thin and taci-
turn, with jet-black hair and deep-set dark eyes, his brown leathery
skin and hooked nose showing his hill-country heritage of moor-
land Saxon, Cornish, Welsh, and Scots seasoned with a dash of
Cherokee, he looked like one of the hard-bitten characters from
the Zane Grey and Louie L'Amour novels he read incessantly. If he
was ever bitter about anything, it was being born too late to be a
character in a Zane Grey novel.

His fly-fishing buddies called him the Grim Reaper, and not
just for his forbidding appearance. One time his friends Joe Bishop

and Sam Kyker were camped up on Bald River and catching nothing when Dad strolled into their camp with a heavy creel. "No wonder we're not catching anything," Joe said. "The damned Grim Reaper's been through here."

As a trout fisherman he was a grim reaper. His short, limber fly rod flashed sidearm like a scythe: three staccato casts with a pair of soft-hackle deer hair wet flies into every likely spot, then on upstream like a wraith, dancing lightly from rock to rock and taking trout after trout.

The summer I was ten we were camped on North River. Dad and Walter, dangerous predators both, had full creels as usual, but I, my head as always in the clouds and my attention wandering everywhere but where I was, had caught only a few horny-head chubs.

After supper I was sitting on the roadside high above Bishop's Bend wondering if I were adopted when Dad materialized downstream. The low rays of the sun at my back lit the scene like a stage, and I could see with the crystal clarity of a PBS nature documentary every movement of rod, line, and fly as Dad took fish from seams, pockets, and riffles; from behind, beside, and in front of rocks; from beneath tangled tree roots and cutbanks; from the surface film to the bottom. I saw how he ghosted close before casting, as invisible as a heron; where he placed his flies, how he avoided drag, when to strike, how to fight a fish. In fifteen minutes I learned more about trout fishing than I had learned in countless hours of frustrating lessons from a teacher too impatient to teach and a pupil too impatient to learn. The scenes recorded like a film, one I replayed over and over in my head that night in the tent, each run-through bringing fresh revelations.

Over a breakfast of leftover trout and horny-heads we formulated the day's plan: Dad and Walter would go high up on

Sycamore Creek after skittish wild browns, and they'd drop me off on the Tellico River where I might luck into a few stupid stocked fish. We'd meet in the late afternoon a few miles upriver.

When I look back on those days I wonder what my mother would have thought had she known Dad routinely deposited her precious little boys along the banks of a rushing mountain river slicing through some of the East's wildest country, with the vague instruction to meet somewhere miles upstream in the late afternoon. These days few parents would risk it; back then it seemed normal.

I sat down to tie on a pair of flies and run one more time through my mind-movie, then I waded out into the quick mountain water. What yesterday had seemed an inscrutable tangle of wild foam and rocks today looked like a connect-the-dots treasure map from a box of Cap'n Crunch. It all seemed so easy: X marks the spot; cast there, drift here, mend the line, strike at the bright flash deep in the current. A fourteen-inch rainbow burst into the air at the tail of the pool, the sun gleaming off the broad scarlet stripe of a streamborn native. Keep the rod tip low and to the side, guide the fish out of the current with relentless sideways pressure. Extend the rod back at arm's length over the shoulder, cushioning the tippet with the rod tip. Now thumb and middle finger into the gills, a quick rap on the head with a knife butt, then into the creel. Creel? When had I ever needed a creel? Okay, into the jeans pocket, headfirst.

On upriver, quick casts into every pool and riffle, playing the movie, *looking* like a trout fisherman. Trouble was, I spent so much time looking like a trout fisherman I forgot to be one. After missing half a dozen strikes in a row I rounded a bend and saw a dark slick of water eddying against a cutbank on the far shore.

Slow down. Remember the movie. Wade carefully across the roaring river, scramble atop a midstream rock, gaining elevation to keep the line out of the main current; cast a few feet above the slick, tossing in an upstream loop of slack just as Dad had done against the eddy at Bishop's Bend. The dropper fly curved and glided into place and disappeared in a fat *bloomp,* then a heavy weight bowed the rod and the line tore out into the heavy current and cut downstream. I hung on and followed, alternately sliding on rocks and falling and swimming and anxiously watching D-level Ashaway line peel off the battered old Ocean City reel. Twenty yards downstream I finally beached a heavy sixteen-inch holdover brown, its bright gold body thickly dotted with crimson and black. A rap on the head and into the other pocket.

Around the next bend I saw the old green Plymouth and my father, sitting on his heel on the riverbank like a mountain man, smoking a cigarette and cleaning a panful of trout. I started across the river toward him and he looked up, his face wreathed in smoke, and began laughing uncontrollably. Who wouldn't at the sight of a scrawny soaked ten-year-old, hopping from rock to rock with a pair of knee-length trout sprouting from his jeans pockets and flapping like wings. Dad yelled up to Walter, "Lord, come see what fish this boy's caught."

He never tired of telling that story: "Me and Walter didn't catch nuthin' but little ol' minners up high on Sycamore Creek, and here come Jimmy a-flappin' across the main river with two big trout and the heads jammed so tight in his pockets I had to cut 'em out with a knife."

I picked him up before daylight at their rented cabin on the foggy Maine coast. Mom and Aunt Nelle were going shopping for pinecone sachets and snowstorm globes filled with lighthouses and plastic lobsters; Dad and I were heading north to fish a pleasant lit-tle brook I'd stumbled on shortly after moving to Maine, a spot where the isolation and the moose and the vistas of Mount Katahdin made the fishing seem better than it really was.

This would be the first time we had exchanged more than a few words in seven years, since he had poured my sorry drunken form into the Trailways bus that took me away for a tour in the navy and some much-needed growing up.

Who knows what biological time bombs trigger mindless teenage rebellion? I sure don't. By high school I no longer went trout fishing in the mountains with Dad and Walter but spent my days in blood-spattered johnboats, drifting globs of shad guts for huge tailrace catfish with my new friends—ne'er-do-well river rats who lived in shanty boats and stayed up all night running trotlines and hunting 'coons and drinking homemade white likker from Mason jars—about as far as you could get from the respectability of the choir, the Rotary Club, the Republican fund-raisers, and the pristine trout streams of the Cherokee National Forest.

After the navy I moved to Boston, where I learned to read literature, learned to edit books, learned I didn't care much for city people, learned all adults were stupid and only my own generation held the keys to wisdom, learned there's more to being a rock-and-roll guitar god than growing hair, pegging a volume control, and grimacing musically. Like scores of other disaffected youth who turned their backs on a world they didn't like and that didn't like them, I went up to the country to grow Swiss chard, practice downward mobility, and postpone adulthood.

We didn't talk about any of this on the long drive north, of course. We just talked about fishing. About the trip to Wyoming and Montana he and Walter had been planning forever, it seemed, and last year had finally made. About the cabin they'd bought up on Riddle Hill behind the old Tellico Lodge, and about how they were fixing it up and moving stuff in from Grandma's old house. About the time he fell off Bald River Falls and came flying out of the water so fast he didn't even get his cigarettes wet—just pulled one nonchalantly from his pocket, scratched a kitchen match with his thumbnail, and lit up, as though he'd meant to fall forty feet into a ten-foot-deep whirlpool just to cool off. About the time when I was eight I'd gone to the mountains camping for two weeks with Aunt Maggie and Uncle Jimmy, and instead of fishing for trout like an honest Babb or my namesake (and unrelated; how many parents name their kids after a fishing buddy?) Uncle Jimmy, I'd spent my time turning over rocks and poking around at bugs and crayfish. About the time I snuck under the safety fence below Fort Loudoun Dam, slipped on the rocks, and got sucked up into the turbine holes, and about how old Willard Parks came up after me in his johnboat and gaffed me like a tuna, and how I still had hold of my stringer of catfish even though I'd lost my glasses and my rod and was more or less dead, and about how the automatic turbine kicked on two minutes after we cleared the boils and about how that would have definitely cleared away the *more or less* in front of *dead* and gotten Willard, too. About the time I'd spent an afternoon treed on top of the Plymouth by a pair of mean-ass Russian hogs before Dad came back from the stream and chased them away with the sassafras-crook gravel flip he'd carried everywhere since he was a kid. About the time we were camped up on Citico Creek when the copperheads were so thick the Fish & Game Department was out killing them on the roads at night. About the time I rock-hopped my way across the main river and got stuck because a copperhead sat coiled on the only rock that could take me to shore, and about how he'd shot its head off at thirty feet with a ball bearing fired from that ever-present slingshot. About the time he caught that monstrous old hook-jawed brown up on North River and Mama was poaching it so proudly with that fancy recipe she'd clipped from *Southern Living,* and how he'd snatched it out of the oven half done and ran outside to show it to his fishing buddy Billy Gilbert, leaving behind a trail of court bouillon across a new green carpet and an apoplectic wife who dove for him at the door like an NFL linebacker and damned near tackled him. And, of course, about my two big trout and that time he'd been really proud of me.

We talked about fishing, as we always had. And we fished as we always had—flipping a coin to see who goes upstream, who goes down. We went our separate ways and we caught trout, and when we met that evening we built a little twig fire and fried them alongside the stream, watching the moose move down to the lake to feed and talking endlessly about fishing: "Try them Swisher-Richards no-hackles yet?"

"Nope. I catch all I want on them old wet flies. Slayed 'em out there in Montanee. Boys you never seen such big trout, or such purty water runnin' through such purty country."

So here I sit in that same spot twenty-three years later, frying trout in the same skillet and wishing I'd known then that rebellion, alienation, and life are all just temporary conditions. I can still see him, sitting on one heel and tending that big iron skillet, humming the bass lines to "A Fountain Filled with Blood" and nursing one of the ever-present Chesterfields that would kill him the following summer at the age of sixty-two.

In three more years he could have met his grandson, seen me finally grow up, become nominally respectable, even get a real job. I could have poured the ultimate coffee addict a cup of La Minita from Costa Rica. Turned the original pepper fiend on to habañeros from Yucatán. Taken him to the West Branch of the Penobscot for explosive landlocked salmon and fished North River with him as an equal.

Instead I sit here by the fire listening to the roar of the stream and thinking about copperheads, two big trout, and the idiocy of youth. Then that line of thinking gets too uncomfortable and, looking for safer terrain, I begin to wonder what would happen if I added a Krystal Flash underwing to an Elk Hair Caddis.

II

New Roots from Old

It is a country full of evergreen trees, of mossy silver birches and watery maples . . . a country diversified with innumerable lakes and rapid streams, peopled with trout . . ., with salmon, shad, and pickerel, and other fishes; the forest resounding at rare intervals with the note of the chickadee, the blue-jay, and the woodpecker, the scream of the fish-hawk and the eagle, the laugh of the loon, and the whistle of ducks along the solitary streams; at night, with the hooting of owls and howling of wolves; in summer, swarming with myriads of black flies and mosquitoes, more formidable than wolves to the white man. Such is the home of the moose, the bear, the caribou, the wolf, the beaver, and the Indian. Who shall describe the inexpressible tenderness and immortal life of the grim forest, where Nature, though it be mid-winter, is ever in her spring, where the moss-grown and decaying trees are not old, but seem to enjoy a perpetual youth; and blissful, innocent Nature, like a serene infant, is too happy to make a noise, except by a few tinkling, lisping birds and trickling rills?

—HENRY DAVID THOREAU, *The Maine Woods*

*T*he wind is picking up, and after the hush of an all-night snow the forest is coming alive: White pine, spruce, fir, and hemlock, stirred into motion by a bright northwesterly chasing away the latest winter low. White pine, spruce, fir, and hemlock. Except for a scattering of big tamaracks and twisted deer apples down by the pond, my office windows look out over an endless expanse of white pine, spruce, fir, and hemlock.

As we drove into the mountains alongside East Tennessee's Tellico River, my father and brother and I would look into its bright pools and pockets with accelerated interest as these harbingers of altitude and latitude began to appear among the tulip poplar and sycamore and oak, marking that amorphous line where smallmouths and redeyes gave way to brown trout then rainbows and, as we moved vertically northward up a tributary and the blue-green spires of spruce and fir began to dominate the mountaintops, brook trout. When we saw that, we knew we were where we wanted to be.

Now, as I look north from my office window into the dense evergreen forest stretching almost unbroken from here to Hudson Bay, then shift my eyes westward to the small pond and the stream beyond where brook trout swim beneath thick gray ice, I know I am where I want to be.

I began moving to Maine when I was twelve years old, after reading and rereading the great Maine-based stories in *Field & Stream* and *Outdoor Life* by Edmund Ware Smith, who lived seven months of the year in a log cabin in Township 6, Range 8, "remote in the Mount Katahdin area, with moose tracks in the dooryard and the nearest telephone twenty-nine miles away"; who went brook trout fishing with One-Eyed Poachers, Supreme Court Justices, and the Enchanted Woodsman, Pappy Thornton, said to be able to start a roaring fire in a downpour with runny cement and two wet sponges. A trip to the library for more about this magic place called Maine turned up but one book: Thoreau's *The Maine*

Woods. This led to a card-catalog search and a seditious little book about independent living and independent thinking called *Walden.* And since twelve is far too young to be reading Thoreau unsupervised, that, as they say, was that.

It took ten more years to get here, with some side trips along the way—navy tours in San Diego and Norfolk, three years in Boston culturing my hair and consciousness—but I had little doubt I'd eventually end up in Maine, especially after I reread as a nominal adult *The Maine Woods* and *Walden* and caught the homesteading fever then running epidemic through the counterculture, and I called up my dad and asked if any homesteaders had shown up around home yet, and he said he'd heard a couple had moved in over to Coker Creek, but that the locals hadn't cottoned to their outlandish ways and had burnt 'em out.

In many ways Mainers are a mirror image of East Tennesseeans—one understated and the other exaggerated; one placid and tolerant and the other volatile and violent; one famously suspicious of strangers and the other openly welcoming, at least on the surface. Ask an East Tennesseean which of these forks in the road goes to Vonore, and he'll happily point you in the right direction, draw you a map, inquire of your health, maybe even invite you onto the porch to set a spell and sip some ice tea. Ask a Mainer if it matters which of these roads you take to Monroe, and he'll probably say, as he turns on his heel and goes back to hoeing his beans, "Not to me it don't." But beyond superficial opposites the people have much in common—English and Scots and a sprinkling of Irish and Germans, with speech patterns and thought processes brought to America centuries ago and still in daily use, retaining in the face of relentless urbanization a deep-seated love for the land and for rural life as the way life should be.

I felt at home in Maine within days of moving here, and after six months I knew I was here to stay.

★   ★   ★

When I drove north from Boston and a failed marriage, I expected to live out my days hermiting around the wild forests north of Bangor—some two-thirds of Maine by area and less than a third by population, so thinly settled more towns have numbers than names, a paradise for someone with a tolerance for blackflies and mosquitoes and an intolerance for anything recognizable as a career that might get in the way of uninterrupted lazing about with books, fly rods, and shotguns. Yet when a thin blond wearing a tube top and a Veronica Lake overbite strolled into the Bangor camera store where I was working and proved to be the funniest and smartest person I'd ever met, somehow I—we—ended up living on the settled Maine coast.

Linda had summered on Deer Isle and needed the sea near her as badly as I needed her near me, but perhaps a bit of coastal come-hither poked through subconscious holes in my genes as well, for in another of those cosmic incongruities that make life entertaining, I ended up earning a living from the ocean for something like twenty years—as a commercial fisherman, a lobster-truck driver, a boatyard worker, a writer about commercial fisheries and boats, an editor of books about boats, ships, and the sea—before finding out that not only had my Babb ancestors gotten their livings from the sea as far back as the twelfth century, but that they had also been among Maine's earliest settlers. On many levels it was as though I had come home.

Linda and I lead a life here in Maine that sounds idealistically organic but, like Thoreau's brief stay at Walden Pond, had its genesis in simple economics: We built a new house because it was cheaper than rebuilding the old house into a semblance of energy efficiency—important in those oil-boycott days. We built it ourselves because we could not afford to have it built by professional house-builders. We bought materials as we had the money and whacked them into place as we had the time because we were happy to trade ten years of inconvenience for thirty years of paying interest. We heat with the sun because it is far cheaper simply to face a wall of glass toward the radiant south, piling thermal mass and insulation and eight feet of earth on the north, east, and west, than it is to conventionally fenestrate a standard-issue box then live in perpetual thrall to an oil dealer. We cook and heat with a woodstove because we can pick up shed tree limbs for free or buy the two cords that take us through a typical year for far less than the equivalent in fossil fuel. We grow our own food because it is cheaper than store-bought food, even considering the cost of our labor and the opportunity cost of time. We sluice the end result of that food into a composting toilet because, with our thin veneer of silty clay over fissured ledge, the elaborate septic system necessary to keep our wastes out of our well would have cost more than the house.

That our house was built from locally produced renewable materials; that it uses a tiny fraction of the energy that fuels a conventional house; that much of that energy is either free or quickly renewable and not pumped from the world's finite supply of fossil fuels; that our homegrown food tastes better than store-bought, not having been marinated in pesticides, herbicides, fungicides, and all the other -cides that ooze insidiously onto supermarket shelves; that the occasional puff of cookstove wood smoke smells better than the skunk-whiff of propane—all are for us important parts of the economic equation as well. Bottom lines are complex and often poorly understood or, worse, purposefully misunderstood. Spending less of your own resources must be balanced with expending more of communal resources. He lives best who impacts least. And if he has a functioning conscience, he sleeps best, too.

I don't mean to imply that we are austere mendicants wallowing in self-righteous deprivation; just that we have learned to earn only what money we need and not what convention says we should have, and what we have earned we spend as we choose, skimping on things some call necessities (ten years with outdoor plumbing, five years with a plastic-bag shower bath) and splurging on things others call luxuries that to us are essential—books, fly rods, shotguns, a decent bottle of wine, good chocolates, and the greatest luxury of all: leisure time.

This is perhaps the most valuable lesson I learned from an early ingestion of Thoreauvian economics and squeezing out, over many years of furrowing my brows while perching on stumps or wandering the woods or casting dry flies to sulfur hatches, my own vision of a proper path through life: Trading time for money is a necessary evil and generally a poor bargain, something I learned firsthand in episodic brushes with careerism during which I could fish only on weekends and not even all of those. Time, like petroleum, is finite, and I will trade any amount of career and its attendant money for unfettered blocks of leisure time, the self-determined freedom to work hard when I wish to work hard and to go fishing when I wish to go fishing. Linda, who teaches art in a village elementary school three days a week and in the other four wanders the woods, reads novels, eats chocolates, and strokes cats, arrived independently at the same conclusion: Like Lord Jim, we have determined to lounge safely through existence.

And for various reasons, among them a writer from the 1950s and another from the 1850s, we are lounging through existence in the State of Maine, fly fishing its uncounted ponds and lakes, streams and rivers, all the while sheltered by the spreading branches and wild spirits of white pine, spruce, fir, and hemlock.

7

A Pond of One's Own

"Personally I think an otter life would be rather enjoyable," continued Laura; "salmon to eat all the year around, and the satisfaction of being able to fetch the trout in their own homes without having to wait for hours till they condescend to rise to the fly you've been dangling before them."

—SAKI, *Beasts and Super-Beasts*

My wife loved the house—one of those ramblingly romantic nineteenth-century sea captain's homes that grace the coast of Maine.

I loved the land. Along its thickly forested back boundary a perfect miniature trout stream sped to the sea. On a perpendicular course, a small spring-seep cut through a steep narrow valley where century-old pines and hemlocks towered over an old dump bleeding thick rusty gouts into cool green moss. On a hilltop overlooking the remains of a log-driving dam, a tiny clearing rimmed by feral rosebushes and gnarled apple trees told of an anonymous vanished homestead. As Linda measured shelf space and peered up chimneys, I walked back to the clearing, leaned against the remains of a Rome Beauty gone wild with water sprouts, and envisioned an earthen dam bulldozed across that close, damp ravine and a shimmering rise-dappled pond swelling behind it.

But in the rush of early familyhood other things took precedence, like building a new house, for the old one quickly taught us why nineteenth-century Mainers like Captain Joshua Walnutt, its original owner, glower from their portraits with dour, embittered faces. Like them, we could travel from the equator to the North Pole merely by trudging a dozen feet from the insatiable woodstove to the bathroom and its frozen plumbing.

After a few rugged years we sold the historic Walnutt House to an innocent young couple afire with Bicentennial nostalgia, kept all the land and a right-of-way to the road, and set about building a new home way back on the hill, a kind of subterranean Hobbit burrow, all timber, stone, and glass, at the interstice of an overgrown potato field and an unbroken forest, one extra utility pole and a thirty-dollar snowplow trip from the nearest neighbor. Twenty-something years later and we're still building, but I never stopped dreaming of the pond we'd build someday—after, of course, I finally wired and sheetrocked the upstairs, built doors and drawers for the kitchen cabinets, replaced the attached greenhouse's milky polyethylene skin with actual glass, and scratched off any number of other gottados from the endless list that grew as rank and unconstrained as the twitch grass besieging our asparagus.

As our new house grew so too did this once woebegone corner of Maine, and as more people built ever more houses, and ever more anglers vied for ever fewer fish, trout appeared ever less often on our menu. This had the intended effect of doing my part to preserve fragile local populations under pressure from less principled predators and the unintended effect of wearing down the first-things-first opposition of a nonfishing budget committee member whose desire for trout on the table finally overcame her desire for a finished kitchen to cook them in. For reasons both economic and ethical, went my argument, we've raised our own broccoli and potatoes, rabbits and lambs. Why not our own trout?

June. The trees are down, the earth scraped bare, the verdant vale an open wound. The old dump, freshly churned by Shawn Stone's bulldozer, reveals the cast-off lives of generations: mangled car parts, liniment bottles, canning jars, pots and pans, Swan Brand Model-T tires, guaranteed puncture-proof. Beneath twisted bedsprings a mouse disconsolately pushes dirt from the remains of its burrow, an earthquake victim clearing away rubble. Tomorrow will bring another temblor, D-6 on the Dozer Scale. Shocking red against blue-green forest, a male cardinal, rare this far north, frantically circles the new clearing, searching for something. I hope it's not home.

But wood ducks will nest here, amphibians will breed. Deer will come to drink and to feed on the rye, clover, and purple vetch that will rim the shores, and when fall comes we will choose one and feed on it. The shallows will fill with wild plants gathered from other ponds of distinction, and through their intertwining leaves legions of scuds and sow bugs, daphnia and copepods will swirl and breed. Fathead minnows will spawn around the stumps, and mayflies and caddis will colonize the mud bottom. Trout will dimple the surface and leap after damselflies. We will have created a fertile oasis in an otherwise sterile climax forest.

Guilt Abatement 101.

July. The dependable thunderstorm cycle is off track this summer, but here and there thin crystal trickles mark the deep boundary between blue and yellow clay, and the sixteen-foot-deep terra-cotta bowl slowly dampens with latte-colored soup already teeming with life. Back swimmers and water striders flit about root wads strategically wired to the bottom. The *gunk* of green frogs punctuates the insistent whine of mosquitoes. Blue-and-grizzly dragonflies dogfight like Spitfires and Messerschmitts over London. Hundreds of unidentifiable plumed invertebrates swirl in formation through the shallows like tiny fan dancers in a Busby Berkeley water spectacular. An osprey beelining for Penobscot Bay and the summer mackerel run spins on one wingtip and dives, a reconnaissance flight that may spell future trouble for future trout. A great blue heron glides silently overhead, stalls, slowly circles, clearly taking notes. *Big* trouble for the trout. But it's been thirty-two days since the last drop of rain, and if we don't get some soon there may be no trout.

September. Still no rain. I've become hooked on the Weather Channel. It's the Days of My Life, As My World Turns. "High pressure holding over northern New England; bright sunny skies continue." *Damn.* "Tropical storms blast the Gulf Coast. Hurricanes menace the Caribbean." *Bugger.*

Tiny green frogs stare up from the dehydrating soup like plaintive little Oliver Twists. Please sir. I want some more. I invite them in to view the Weather Channel. A helicopter plucks a screaming woman from atop her car drowning in a Deep South parking lot. *Lucky Bastards.*

It's official: This is the worst drought in 125 years. Extreme Fire Danger! the forest service warns for the first time since the wildfires of 1939. Tourists fleeing city heat, mopping their brows and choking on smoke from a million-acre forest fire burning out of control upwind in Quebec, complain as though lured here under false pretenses. Worried fisheries biologists replace ruined potato farmers on the local news. Rivers are down to half their normal flow, they tell us, and the fisheries may not recover for years. A quarter inch of ineffectual rain fell last night, and the pond is down to a skim of syrupy ooze. The frogs are disgusted and so am I.

November. And the rains came. Last month, after causing more damage than any storm since Andrew, Hurricane Opal came screeching up the Appalachian basin and spewed four inches of rain across the northeast, the first significant rainfall since May. Since then we've had a major rain and wind event, as the local TV-weather geeks say, almost every week—hurricane-force winds, torrential rains, trees down everywhere, major flooding, lowland evacuations, shelters open, insurance agents unplugging their telephones, the worst power outages since Hurricane Bob. The water's now a foot and half below the spillway and rising fast. More importantly, area streams and rivers are running to capacity. I tour the spawning beds of a dozen nearby streams and to my relief see trout carrying on the age-old dance of procreation. The Northeast's fishing has been wounded, but it appears not fatally.

December. When water finally began flowing down the spillway it seemed somehow anticlimactic, for now the thermometer plummets and the snow begins, and after barely a week as a Real Pond it has gelled into an ice sculpture. The tracks of deer, foxes, raccoons, and mink crisscross its frozen surface. A great horned owl glares from the Big Tree, a giant Siamese twin of pine and fir growing from interspecial roots. For less than the price of a beater used car, an unused corner of our backyard has become the most pleasant place I know on earth. Why did we wait so long?

January. And the storms rage on. By New Year's we had received sixty-two of the sixty-seven inches of snow we're allotted for the entire winter, and temperatures dived far below normal. Then in mid-January a long line of coastal depressions queuing at four-day intervals firehosed away all the snow. Rivers and streams statewide are again in flood—evacuations on the Kennebec and Penobscot, ice dams forming everywhere. Freakish southerly winds destroyed the town wharf—a not insubstantial structure of oak pilings and quarried granite blocks the size of mini vans. It's a Wrath of God winter to complement our Wrath of God summer. What's next: Boils? Serpents?

March. And so the slow unlocking begins. Most of the winter's 120 inches of snow—twice the normal amount—is gone, and the ground has that loathsome mud-season consistency of institutional pudding. Moose tracks pock the dam's soft corner—perhaps a young bull prospecting for a refuge against the summer blackfly onslaught. As we learned in countless episodes of *Bullwinkle,* the moose may look dumb, but in the end he's usually right: This *is* a superb retreat, and as the spillway thickens with runoff I begin to build a small frame office, a spillway in its own right channeling the overflow of fishing books, fishing equipment, fishing activities, fishing work from the crowded, noisy house to this quiet spot overlooking the pond. A refuge of my own. A fish-writer's paradise. A tax deduction.

May. A ton of agricultural lime exchanges ions with the suspended clay and magically sends it to the bottom. The pea soup algae slowly clarifies; the black-and-white Secchi disk remains visible at six feet. Life blooms everywhere—water striders, back swimmers, water boatmen. Two mammoth lantern beetles mate like Volkswagens in a freeway mishap. And now the pond receives its raison d'être: 120 six-inch trout—rainbows, alas, the hatchery having run out of brook trout, but at least they're trout. With this it finally becomes a real pond, for a pond without rising fish is merely a stagnant pool.

July. Shades of Turok Son of Stone—the comic-book Plains Indian chased across 1950s pulp pages by an incongruous array of saber-toothed tigers, tyrannosaurs, and pterodactyls—especially ptero-dactyls. "Aieeeeee," Turok's sidekick would wail in episode after episode as a great winged lizard whisked him away. "Aieeeeee," Turok would agree, futilely launching a stone-tipped arrow. But like all good comic-book heroes, Turok always won in the end and freed his companion from, depending on your viewpoint, either a rapacious predator laying waste the countryside or an oppressed single parent scraping up a family meal. Would that I were so intre-pid a champion as Turok. Or so skilled a predator as a pterodactyl's lineal descendent, the great blue heron.

Daybreak finds me in bathrobe and Bean boots, stalking a modern-day pterodactyl that, in little more than a month, has gulped down something like half our trout. I flit noiselessly from bush to bush, slingshot in hand and terrycloth flapping in the breeze, clouds of mosquitoes enjoying my pantlessness. But long before I'm in position to fire the heron spots me and flaps disdain-fully into the air.

I'm not out to commit murder, especially not of a federally pro-tected species. I just want to scare the homesteading instinct out of this heron before I'm left with one lonely rainbow quivering in midpond.

Are my scare tactics working? Last night I eased out to the pond and found three herons placidly wading the shallows. *Aieeeeee!*

August. I've waited twenty years and can wait no longer. It's time to eat some guilt-free trout before the herons get them all, or at least those too numb to avoid the narrow band of shallow, heron-haunted water. Linda makes an extravagant salad and bakes baguettes. I heat clarified butter in the skillet, string up a four-weight, and head for the pond.

From the low peninsula where each morning I toss trout kibbles, a farmer feeding his flock, I cast a deer hair sculpture of a chunk of Flyte Floating Fish Food and . . . nothing. I cast again and again. Nothing. I toss in a few kibbles for chum and they're smashed instantly, the trout bombing straight up and diving like yo-yos. Several flash at my fake Flyte, one even bumps it with his nose, but they all turn away in disinterest.

I once said trout aren't smart. I now formally recant. Even feed-lot rainbows know real food when they see it.

An hour later Linda wanders back to ask if the butter is meant to be black and smoking. I snarl something unpleasant and go back to chumming with kibbles. The trout are beating the water to a froth and so am I. Only they're eating, and it doesn't look like we will.

I head for the garden, grabbing the spading fork en route. Worms. Back at the pond I quickly connect with two fat silver rainbows—flashing leapers like all their tribe. We'll eat tonight, but my supper goes down with a healthy serving of crow. Forty years a fly fisherman? Bah.

Autopsies reveal stomachs packed like sausages with, by volume, 60 percent kibbles, 20 percent rye seeds (!), and 20 percent miscellaneous insects, almost all various chironomids—pupae, larvae, and adults, in that order.

I either need a better kibble imitation or some crackerjack midges. I head for the tying vise, a copy of Darrel Martin's

Micropatterns clutched in humbled palm and a saucerful of stomach gleanings at the ready. The next day, a half-dozen size 24 shucking midge pupae in hand, I head for the pond and the moment of truth.

In *Spring Creek,* Nick Lyons writes that he doesn't want more trout or bigger trout but harder trout, and he found them on an anonymous western creek flush with feed and huge, hyperselective wild fish. I found mine in my backyard, flush with little hatchery trout packed with kibbles and midge pupae, fish that learned all they need to know about predation from the local heronry. I learned a bit myself, watching a heron feed one evening, defining stolid persistence in ways a heavy ice tea drinker can never hope to emulate.

At dusk, after a spiral of ever stealthier tactics, I finally take two fish on a minuscule midge pupa, a twelve-foot, 6X leader, and a sixty-foot cast.

Trout for supper. I could not be more proud.

As I turn for the house, dinner in hand, two herons spiral slowly overhead—real anglers waiting patiently for the dub amateur to clear the pool. I pick my way across the dam and see below, in the soft clay thinly garnished with sprouting clover, fresh otter tracks leading into the pond, and the gnawed remnants of a little silver rainbow.

Aieeeeee.

8

In the Wake of Henry D.

*There stood Ktaadn with distinct and cloud-
less outline in the moonlight; and the rippling
of the rapids was the only sound to break the
stillness. Standing on shore, I once more cast
my line into the stream, and found the dream
to be real and the fable true.*

—HENRY DAVID THOREAU,
The Maine Woods

Transcendentalist, naturalist, visionary, wilderness flautist—
Henry David Thoreau was all these things and one other: He
was Maine's first real tourist, the first white man to come to these
damp, dour woods purely to drink in their wild tang and not to
scout for sawmill fodder or inhabitants to slaughter and/or evange-
lize. The chronicles of his three trips, in 1846, 1853, and 1857, are
collected in *The Maine Woods*, a brilliantly evocative volume partly

87

to blame for my moving here and for Maine's annual incursion of Vacationlanders, at least that small portion who prefer an unadulterated slice of North Woods to the heavily salted commercial coastal edition.

Its 1864 publication, complete with a recommended "Outfit for an Excursion" that included sixteen pounds of pork and twelve of sugar and the caution that "if you take an Indian and canoe at Oldtown, it will cost seven or eight dollars more to transport them to the lake," brought increasing numbers of would-be wilderness mystics to the Maine woods in search of what Thoreau found: a "stern, yet gentle, wildness on my memory as will not soon be effaced." He meant it, too, for when Thoreau lay dying of tuberculosis in 1862, his final sentence contained only two intelligible words: "Indian" and "moose."

Within twenty years Thoreau's "grim, untrodden wilderness, whose tangled labyrinth of living, fallen, and decaying trees only the deer and moose, the bear and wolf can easily penetrate," had sprouted a full-blown tourist industry, catering to a growing flow of urbanites caught up in the era's back-to-nature movement. Before corporate America found other uses for our leisure time, families of means came here every summer for a month or more of loafing, fishing, and rusticating at luxurious wilderness retreats. Nowhere were these resorts more concentrated or elegant than around the shores of Moosehead Lake—"a perfect lake of the woods," wrote Thoreau, "seen over the infant port of Greenville with mountains on each side and far in the north, and a steamer's smoke-pipe rising above the roof."

On his trips to Chesuncook Lake and the West Branch of the Penobscot, and to the Allagash and the East Branch, Thoreau passed twice through Greenville, once sharing a stagecoach with fellow wilderness flute player Hiram Leonard, then a celebrated hunter and gunsmith and not yet the proud father of the hexagonal split-cane rod. Then as now Greenville was the gateway to the North Woods, and were he to drive down Indian Hill on the old Bangor road today, Thoreau would still recognize the scene. Except for a gleaming new McDonald's and an embryonic strip mall blighting the approach, Greenville seems from another age—a hospitable nineteenth-century village sparingly spackled with a pastiche of 1950s tourist-trap, 1970s artsy-crafty, and 1990s commerce.

In the old days summer people arrived by rail, and a fleet of fifty steamboats ferried gossamer-garbed belles and stiff-collared dandies to Capen's Island Hotel or the five-hundred-room Kineo House. Now T-shirted tourists arrive by automobile and only the steamer *Katahdin* remains, still cruising gracefully up the forty-mile-long lake to Mount Kineo, a forbidding mass of Lower Devonian rhyolite that furnished northeastern Indians with arrowheads and the legend from which Moosehead Lake derives its name.

It was here, go the tales, that a mighty Abenaki hunter slew the Queen of the Moose Tribe, whose head and body can still be seen in Kineo and its connecting peninsula. In pre-European days the moose was the cornerstone of the economy, furnishing food, clothing, and shelter, and "God's own horses" are just as important to the local economy today. The first question wide-eyed visitors to Greenville ask is, "Where can I see a moose?" The answer is practically everywhere. In the millions of acres of timberlands "all mossy and moosey" surrounding Greenville, it's almost impossible *not* to see a moose. Or moose T-shirts, moose coffee cups, moose statues, and moose-turd jewelry.

One night, driving slowly back to Greenville along the eastern shore of Moosehead Lake after a transcendental evening of catching bright red brook trout from float tubes in tiny mountaintop

Bluff Pond with Dan Legere, a Maine guide and something of a local legend himself, we saw seven of Moosehead's totem animals. Dan pulled the truck over as a pair of parentally banished yearling bulls lumbered into the forest. He leaned out the window, cupped his hands, and, like Thoreau's guide many years before, grunted "nOOOOnwuh, nOOOOnwuh, nOOOOnwuh." The two moose spun around and jogged toward the truck. "Come on back home, boys," Dan called out as they drew near. "Mommy still loves you and all is forgiven." They skidded to a stop then disappeared into the woods, looking over their shoulders like "great frightened rabbits, with their long ears and half-inquisitive, half-frightened looks." Innocents betrayed. A few days later, while looking for a way into the Upper Pleasant River via a spider's web of run out tote roads a few miles from town, I saw two foxes, nine deer, a bear, and, in the middle of a rough two-track near a log yard, two fishers (*Martes pennanti,* not the gender-neutral term for fishermen) frantically coupling—a sight beyond rare, the very face of wild.

It's astonishing, in this day and age, just how wild Maine really is, and equally astonishing that its wildness owes less to intentional conservation than to commerce. Maine is the nation's most heavily forested state because much of it is a giant, privately owned paper plantation—a huge tree factory spinning out endless miles of toilet paper, paper towels, your Sunday paper, and the pages of this book. Thoreau worried that timber interests would destroy this wilderness. Ironically, it was they who preserved it, though for how much longer remains to be seen, as publicly traded new logging companies with no local ties and a history of stripping timberlands then selling the cutover remains as recreational properties buy up Maine's great North Woods at an unprecedented rate.

"In the night I dreamed of trout-fishing," Thoreau wrote, "and, when at length I awoke, it seemed a fable that this painted fish swam there so near my couch, and rose to our hooks the last evening, and I doubted if I had not dreamed it all." Then and now, the brook trout, those "bright fluviatile flowers . . . made beautiful, the Lord only knows why, to swim here!" are Maine's most popular and widespread fish, but to hardcore anglers, especially fly fishers, the most precious is the landlocked salmon. The product of ancient glacial isolation, landlocks are essentially identical to Atlantic salmon and share most of their habits, including a violently aerobatic and roving nature. But unlike Atlantics, which do not feed in fresh water, landlocks seem never to stop eating, cruising endlessly in search of food and not, like trout, lying in wait for it. And they grow *big*—the state record, set in 1907, is twenty-two and a half pounds. These days the typical salmon averages only fifteen to eighteen inches, but in choice spots fish to five or six pounds are not uncommon. I lack the talent to describe a landlock's fight, but having caught both I'll lay real money that an eighteen-inch river-born salmon could stomp a mud hole in a twenty-four-inch brown with both pectorals tied behind its back.

The Moose and Roach Rivers and the East Outlet of Moosehead, part of the headwaters of the Kennebec River, can offer fast fishing for landlocks, as can the Rapid and Kennebago in western Maine and Grand Lake Stream down east. But two miles across Northeast Carry from Moosehead Lake lies the West Branch of the Penobscot, with perhaps the best landlocked salmon fishing in the world. Over the years I've followed Thoreau's wake up and down its length, often fishing and camping at the mouths of Ragmuff and Pine Streams above Chesuncook Lake, where the Penobscot is little more than a gentle and lonely trout stream and where Thoreau fished and botanized and "sucked at the very teat's of nature's pine-clad bosom." Below Ripogenus Dam, however, the West Branch becomes a brawny, brawling tailwater, with massive hatches of caddis, stoneflies, mayflies, and, unfortunately, white-water rafters.

One man's wilderness is another's ride at Coney Island, and for a dozen or more years after the white-water rafting industry showed up in the mid-1970s and essentially took over the river, I avoided the West Branch altogether. But a few years ago I became friends with Will Ryan after editing his book on smallmouth fishing, and he convinced me that, given the quality of the fishing, the flotillas of whooping rafters can be nearly bearable, especially in the evening when the rafters abandon the river to cluster around campfires and stare into the flames, singing campfire songs, thrilling to their adventurous natures, and trying to get laid. Besides, like Atlantic salmon fishing and unlike brook trout fishing, landlock fishing has long been a more or less communal sport, with anglers clustered fifty feet to port and starboard of one another in name-brand pools like Big Eddy, Little Eddy, Steep Bank, Holbrook, Nesowadnehunk Deadwater. Given this, a careening Avon full of screeching Bostonnais becomes little more than a colorful albeit annoying background.

Landlock fishing is synonymous with the classic Maine streamers—Gray Ghost, Nine-Three, Barnes Special, Kennebago Smelt. But landlocks don't just chase the rainbow smelt these flies imitate; in the right hands weighted stonefly nymphs are the most deadly lures of all, especially if tipped with eighteen inches of 5X and a tiny PT or caddis emerger. And salmon spend a great deal of their time scanning the surface. One June I was sitting on a rock with Tom Fuller, watching Will across the West Branch pound his outsize marabou streamers into a horserace, when the Parachute Hare's Ear I was idly dapping on the surface disappeared in a beaver-alarm *kah-PLOONK,* the rod tip snapped below the surface, the old Beaudex cut loose with a frightening banshee squall, and a melon-shaped salmon some two feet long leaped three times head-high, shaking his head like a tarpon, and from no more than six feet away at the apex of his hang time spat the fly straight back in my face. Tom and I, both in our prime heart-attack years, shook our heads, too, and vented a stream of fine old Anglo-Saxon invective. You can endure a lot of white-water rafters for even the briefest of encounters with a fish like that.

Endurance is itself the key to fishing Maine. Along with the unpredictable weather come unimaginable numbers of tiny, bloodthirsty blackflies, which like Africa's tsetse flies do a fine job of thinning out human populations (as does the officially recognized highest cost of living in the U.S. when income is figured in). Thoreau came here twice in the fall and once in late July, well past the worst of blackfly season. Although he calls Maine's blackflies "more formidable than wolves to the white man," this lacks the ring of true experience, so I'll purloin the notes of a Recollet lay brother who in the early seventeenth century traveled nearby in the very height of the season, mid-June: "So pestiferous and poisonous are the bites of these little demons," he wrote, that "they make one look like a leper, hideous to the sight. I confess that this is the worst martyrdom I suffered in this country; hunger, thirst, weariness, and fever are nothing to it."

The blackflies would be nearly bearable if they worked alone, but when they punch out at sundown limitless squadrons of mosquitoes come on duty. Taking over at midnight and staying industrious until morning are clouds of no-see-ums and their bites of festering heat. At daybreak the blackflies come back on the job and are assisted throughout the day by an endless procession of deer- and moose flies, which attack silently from astern with bites like jabs from soldering irons.

Dan Legere tells prospective clients up front: "If bugs bother you, don't come." And a lot don't, but Mainers don't miss them. We just slather on the bug dope and rain gear and head for the still-wild Maine woods. Some things are worth any amount of hard-ship, at least to me, for when I look around at this place I have chosen to live out my days, I feel in my bones what Thoreau felt when he wrote, "What a place to live, what a place to die and be buried in! There certainly men would live forever, and laugh at death and the grave."

9

Alone on a
Nameless Stream

*I have never found the companion that was so
companionable as solitude. We are for the most
part more lonely when we go abroad among
men than when we stay in our chambers.*

—HENRY DAVID THOREAU, *Walden*

I know a man in love with a tiny nameless creek a six-hour
plane ride from his hectic New York office. When he isn't
there he dreams about it; when he is there he's in a dream. It holds
plenty of browns and some big ones, too, though nothing like the
monsters found in name-brand rivers nearby. Like many small
streams, its power to fascinate lies less in its fish than in its fishing—
its unspoiled surroundings, its intimate scale, its perfect solitude.

Four hours by car or boat in any direction from my office is
some of the best fishing in the East. Anglers from around the world

95

come for the Atlantic salmon of the Miramichi, the landlocks of the West Branch, the brook trout of the Rangeleys, the smallmouths of the Penobscot, the stripers and bluefish of the Kennebec, the swordfish and makos and giant bluefin tuna of the Gulf of Maine.

There's enough great fishing to keep anyone busy for a lifetime. But as years go by I find myself returning to my youth, spending ever more time chasing herring-size trout on nameless little streams. Two dozen beckon within a half hour's drive, but my favorite is only a sixty-second walk from my office door—two miles of thin, tannin-stained pocket water hurrying over a narrow, twisting bed of granite and gravel toward its rendezvous with a thin arm of the Atlantic ocean.

I fish it only four or five times a season, its sparse population of brook trout too fragile to be endlessly caught and released like toys. But throughout the year I walk its length almost daily, watching it, sitting by it, prying into its secrets with eyes, not nymphs, muttering to it like Tolkien's Gollum: Yesssss, my preciousss. What has it got in its pocketsesss? Nice little fishesss, yesssss.

Soon after the spring freshets and the attendant run of meat fishermen subside, I have this little stream and its many neighbors all to myself, just me and the trout and the bugs and an occasional moose driven south by blackflies and tourists. Twenty years ago, well before fly fishing's recent growth spurt, I shared these small neighborhood streams with scores of other fly fishers—quiet, reflective anglers for whom small-stream fishing formed the philosophic core of their sport. Now, what was once holy water held in common by a tight-knit fly-fishing community is the haunt only of children and eccentric mutterers. Today's fly fishers flock in raucous collegiate groups to blue-ribbon waters and fish elbow to elbow with the rapacious fury of Wall Street bond traders—"whackin' 'em, rippin' lips"—seemingly less interested in experiencing the wilderness than in having experiences in the wilderness. And looking good doing it.

*   *   *

Maybe that's what still draws a few of us to the lonely places. Free from crowds and the pressure to perform for our peers, we can relax and immerse ourselves in the fish's world without worrying that our loops are lumpy or our flies undone. No matter how fashionably attired or splendidly equipped, you simply cannot look good fishing small streams. In most places a long cast is twenty-five feet, usually sidearmed inelegantly from a kneel or a squat. Often there's nothing recognizable as casting at all, just flipping—a short, sharp, diagonal slash of the wrist with an abrupt midair stop, like a truncated Spey cast. Done correctly, the fly alights intuitively right where you're looking. Or so goes the theory.

In the days before fly-fishing schools made instant if sometimes superficial experts of everyone, most of us caught our first trout on small streams—perfect little scale models of big rivers, complete in every detail. The full-immersion baptism in a miniature, self-contained ecosystem taught us not only how to fly fish for trout, but why we would want to.

Streams like these have never seen a hatchery truck, and are home to wild strains of trout as regionally distinctive as accents before TV made us all talk like Californians. My stream, proprietarily speaking, has two distinct races of brook trout: a pastel fish that in high water and equinoctial tides commutes to the ocean over an old milldam, and a coal-black group of stay-at-homes with neon red spots that glow like stoplights beneath the hemlocks. A few miles to the east is a beaver-meadow stream with an olive-green strain of brookies covered with intricate, M. C. Escheresque vermiculations cut by a broad swath of fluorescent orange. Just to the northwest, in a little farm-country brook winding through pastures and cornfields, lives a mutant race of thick-bodied trout already *au bleu*.

None of these streams are nameless, of course, but revealing the name and therefore whereabouts of an obscure little stream with pleasant fishing is the work either of a fool or the truest friend who ever was. The best small streams are those you find on your own—meandering alone down country roads, large-scale maps spread across the seat, a rod and hip boots at the ready; nowhere special to go, just looking for water and solitude. You appreciate more what you have worked hardest to find. And you keep it to yourself.

Excepting the pampered inhabitants of spring creeks, small-stream trout lead hardscrabble lives. Regular floods and droughts make reproduction iffy, and unprincipled predation quickly decimates populations. My own predatory principles are based in part on biology and in part on the diameter of my favorite iron skillet. Thus each year I take no more than five trout from any given body of water that I know to be healthy and lightly fished, none smaller than eight inches (the threshold of full flavor development) or larger than nine and a half, in part because they won't fit in the skillet without beheading and thus losing that tasty nibble of cheek, and in part because killing larger trout is shortsighted plundering of very shallow gene pools. And I don't fish for any species during spawning season for the same reason I disapprove of hitting on women in maternity wards: It's just tacky.

Specialized fly tackle is available for every purpose these days, but you really don't need much for small-stream fishing: a small box of assorted flies, a few tippet spools and a spare leader or two, nippers, forceps, fly flotant, bug dope—it all fits in shirt pockets or hangs off your belt.

Creeping close to skittish trout means you must wear drab or even camouflage clothing and genuflect deeply and often. This knee-dipping pilgrimage wears through your own knees as quickly as it does hip boots, and I've taken to stitching multiple layers of dead blue jeans to the quick-drying nylon pants I wear wet-wading and, for cold days, choosing hip boots with built-in pads or sticking on truck-tube knee patches with a smear of Aquaseal.

I'm not sure the perfect small-stream rod exists, though people with more money than me swear it's a Paul Young Driggs River Special, a seven-foot, two-inch five-weight designed specifically for firing bushy dry flies under bushes. The last one I saw on a used-rod list carried an eighteen-hundred-dollar price tag, about what I paid for my last pickup truck. I've been allowed to cast a friend's Driggs, though only under close supervision and never in the stream. Even on a lawn I felt the Driggs might be The One, though with a half-finished house and a son headed for college I don't see one coming my way anytime soon.

In a lifetime of searching for The One True Rod I've accumulated a considerable stable of pretty good pretenders, and before heading out for a day of backwater solitude I rifle through the rack like a teenager dressing for a date. If I'm feeling retro and casting multiple wet flies on a short line I may take a seven-foot four-weight Shakespeare Wonderod I've had since I was twelve. For short-range firing of aerodynamically incorrect dry flies I grab a tip-heavy seven-and-a-half-foot five-weight Orvis Battenkill from the Wes Jordan era that loads with only a foot of line out and has become over the years an extension of my arm. For tunnel fishing—crawling through tangles of interlocking alders after large skittish fish—there's my dad's three-piece six-foot six-weight Berkley Parametric from the early 1960s that will launch a big beetle in a straight line like a wrist rocket and jerk the eyeteeth out of a bad-ass black-water brown. For the thin waters of August, when anything more threatening than a Lilliputian ant fluttering to the surface sends trout speeding for cover, I used to fish a weepy old seven-foot three-weight Montague—a poor man's Leonard 38L, or so I tried to convince myself—but I've recently taken a shine to the new generation of ultralight one- to three-weight graphite rods from makers like Green River, Thomas & Thomas, and Sage. And don't discount fiberglass. Among new rods are Scott's splendid little Fibertouch small-stream specials, and used fiberglass rods perfect for small waters are available for pocket change; small Fenwicks and Scientific Anglers' "System" rods come to mind. And there are Stradivarii in glass as well as in cane; if you happen across any small fiberglass rods labeled RUSS PEAK or VINCE CUMMINGS, you have struck gold.

The point is, almost anything can work as a small-stream rod providing it's between six and a half and seven and a half feet long, balances with a three- to five-weight line, and bends more than is currently fashionable with the sixty-feet-of-line-out crowd. You need something designed to cast, as A. J. McClane wrote in *Field & Stream* way back before small-stream fishing fell from fashion with très cool anglers, "a light line, long, fine leaders, and small flies" to a "1-pound trout poised on nervous fins not 40 feet away"; a rod that can hold "20-30 feet of line in the air without the need for excessive casting speed." One that has "a slow casting cycle so you have control of the fly and the line displays no tendency to drop prematurely." Though thirty years old, McClane's comments still precisely describe the perfect rod for small waters. Note that this rules out modern fast-action graphite rods, which are designed less to cast line than to shoot it.

Boiled down: When shopping for a small-stream rod, head for the parking lot to see not how far it will cast but how short it will cast easily and with control. Because the best small-stream fishing always requires walking farther than other anglers are prepared to do, a three- or four-piece rod that straps easily to a day pack is a definite plus; lump obsessionists who claim multipiece rods don't cast as well as two-piece rods with the princess who always felt the pea no matter the number of intervening mattresses. And although few prosthetics carry more sensual eye appeal than a fly rod, a glowing finish garnished with bright shining ferrules and guides quickly telegraphs your presence to wary trout. Like the lethal tools of all slippery stalkers, a good small-stream rod reflects little or no light.

Weight-forward lines are better than double tapers on small streams; you want as much weight outside the guides as you can get, and I often overline a size if I know I'll be casting short. Reels don't matter in the least. I favor the same old Pflueger Medalists and J. W. Young Beaudexes I've been using forever. Scrambling around a small stream will quickly trash a complex, finely machined reel, and you'll find no occasion to wish for a disk drag. Think simple and durable.

For most fishing, your leader should be no longer than your rod. Few knotless leaders have enough butt to turn over a fly with only a few feet of line out, so you'll probably have to roll your own. Of the many different small-stream leader recipes I've tried over the years, the best came from Charles Meck's *Fishing Small Streams with a Fly Rod*: eighteen inches of .015, twelve inches of .013, eight inches of .012, six inches of .010, four inches of .008, and twenty-two inches of .007. I usually leave the tag end of the .008 section about six inches long for a dry-fly dropper—an alternative far superior to strike indicators for small-water nymphing.

Fly selection has become a science, but on small freestone streams it's still impressionist art. Hatches tend to be multiple and sporadic, and fish feed opportunistically or not at all. You'll need only a couple of generic nymphs, a few soft-hackle wets, some attracter-style dries, a terrestrial of some sort, and a selection of small Woolly Buggers. Anything else is just showing off. My small-stream fly box changes with seasons and whims, but it always features a Devil Bug—an old Adirondack pattern of spartan simplicity, consisting only of a dubbed fur or herl body, a little deer hair lashed on tips-aft just above the barb then pulled forward, tied off behind the eye, and trimmed to a 1950s brush cut: it looks like a Humpy astonished at finding itself with no hackle. A Devil Bug can be fished dry, wet, or stripped as a streamer—sometimes all three in the same cast, and it makes a grand strike indicator for a tiny soft-hackle wet fly.

Small-stream fishing is trout fishing reduced to its essence. There's only you and the fish, and they're a very critical audience. Trout grown large enough to become interesting got that way by sensing the presence of predators before predators sensed them, and if you don't dress in colors that match the background and haven't learned to wade as carefully as a heron you'll catch only the smallest and dumbest fish in the water. This holds true on large rivers as well, but there you could blame your skunking on no fish or atmospheric conditions or the wrong fly or even, all too often in these days of escorted fishing expeditions, on your guide. On a small stream you have no one to blame but yourself, and the consequences of your errors are readily visible and invariably instructive.

If you can't cast accurately you will catch few fish. Form, style, lovely tight loops—none of it matters if you can't drop your fly soundlessly into a dishpan twenty-five feet away, sidearming the rod parallel to the water. This too is a portable lesson that will serve you well on larger waters, where despite the emphasis on casting for distance the best fish are probably only thirty feet away and can plainly see your rod flashing back and forth high in their portable viewing windows.

Although some small streams can hold surprisingly large fish, they're more likely to average between six and eleven inches. If that sounds insignificant compared with a two-foot hog wrenched from the Big Hole, it is. That's the point. Being alone on a nameless stream isn't really about catching fish. It's about fishing.

10

Against the Grain

From childhood's hour I have not been
As other were—I have not seen
As others saw.

—EDGAR ALLAN POE, "Alone"

We sat together, my dad and I, waiting for a Trailways bus to come haul me over the Cumberland Mountains to Nashville and the U.S. Navy's induction center.

"Jimmy," he said, with the ponderous gravity of a father bestowing the gift of timeless ancestral wisdom on a son going bravely forth into the wide world of adulthood. "At least try to *act* normal."

I've tried, but I don't know how well I've succeeded.

Like most people, my brain is split down the middle into a left lobe, which is linear and logical and insists we eat our vegetables and go to work on time, and a restively rebellious right lobe that wants us to call in sick and go fishing, picking up a Moon Pie and a Yoo-Hoo on the way.

For better or worse, my right lobe has won most of those arguments.

Even when engaged in such relentlessly right-brain activities as fly fishing, I'm as easily distracted as a three-year-old. If I had a dollar for every time I've diverted my glassy gaze from copulating damselflies to find my dry fly cutting a V-wake fifty feet downstream, I wouldn't need to go to work at all.

Over the years I've gotten better at temporarily partitioning off the right lobe so the left side can earn enough to keep us in Yoo-Hoos and Moon Pies, but it's been a long and winding road.

Like most folks', my left lobe is an editor, peering peevishly over half-glasses as it purses its lips and briskly taps its blue pencil, tsk-tsk-tsking at the antics of its loopy cranialmate and hacking unfettered imagination into a semblance of structured logic. In one of those cosmically weird improbabilities that ensures truth is always stranger than fiction, this is how I've earned my living these past twelve years.

During the seven years I spent editing books from eight to five in an office a thirty-two-mile commute into Midcoast Maine's high-rent district, I worried that my right lobe's habit of staring vacantly out the window at the birdies and squirrels while deadlines were crashing all around would goad my left lobe into permanently partitioning it off, as Montresor did unto Fortunato in Poe's "The Cask of Amontillado"—especially after a multinational corporation accidentally bought the tiny Maine boating-book publisher I was working for and dragged it and its tight-knit staff kicking and screaming into a Machiavellian corporate world that made *Dilbert* look like *The Family Circus*.

Fortunately, my right lobe, along with other grumbling body parts, convinced me to bail out, career be damned, and in the five years since that I've earned a sort of living editing and writing in a ramshackle little office out behind the house, they've maintained an uneasy peace, the left side agreeing to allow the right side its whimsical interruptions and the right side agreeing to stop calling the left side an inflexible pissant.

Not that I don't still wander.

For instance, while writing this chapter, which in a fly-fishing sense is meant to chart "the measure of my perversities," as Leeson put it when helping me think through the rationale behind this thing and which in typical nonlinear fashion is being written last although it goes in the middle of a book already two weeks overdue at the publisher, I happened to look toward the office floor for inspiration and spied a couple of tiny flies coughed up by the dust bunnies—a pale olive beadhead caddis pupa and a Pheasant Tail, both about size 20. I got down on my hands and knees and started poking around in the dust looking for more flies, found two, then I headed up to the house for a foxtail and a dustpan, decided to make a cup of coffee and check my e-mail, and became entangled in a burst of free-associative Websurfing that began with a simple Internet search for a little something extra to season chapter 11— somehow I'd convinced myself that Pleistocene beavers the size of Volkswagens had constructed the Great Plains, and that readers of a book having nothing to do with the Great Plains or the things found thereon might find this interesting—and ended after learning far more about gynecological anomalies than anyone should who has innocently typed the words *giant beavers* into an Internet search engine. Then I went back out to the office and swept the floor, sifting through the detritus and netting a half-dozen tiny assorted flies, whose source I finally traced to the vest that I'd been meaning to hang up since winter shut down fly fishing three months ago but which had gotten no farther in its journey toward the closet than sprawling damply across the unabridged dictionary. After finding a wool drying patch still shedding flies, I started stuffing them back into the appropriate boxes, then remembered I'd been meaning to reorganize my vest for the past three years, so I spread out everything and starting moving stuff around into what seemed like a logical needs-based assortment, then I remembered that those tiny olive beadhead caddis pupae were what Lepage and I had caught all those brook trout and salmon on at the East Outlet last October, but I only had one well-chewed specimen left and I couldn't remember how I'd tied them, so I went for Darrel Martin's *Micropatterns* to see if I'd marked the pertinent page, but since I still haven't gotten around to reorganizing the bookshelves I somehow found myself taking down the 1904 edition of Fannie Hardy Eckstrom's *The Penobscot Man*, and I started leafing through it because I couldn't remember what Eckstrom had written about Joe Attien, Thoreau's guide on his first trip, and I thought I might find a good quote and maybe a new slant for the chapter on Thoreau's Maine that I'd finished reworking three months before but still wasn't that happy with, but then I got distracted by a neat story called "A Clump of Poseys" about the author's adventures as the sole woman among 174 men on a West Branch log drive, and when I finished that I went outside to pee and started clearing snow off the canoe, wondering how the almost-finished seat caning was faring in this winter's wild temperature and humidity swings, and I found a similar but better-preserved beadhead caddis pupa stuck in the canoe's rail and wandered back into the office to tie some for the blank spots in the fly boxes. Then, because I still couldn't remember how I'd tied them, I went for *Micropatterns* again and found something similar only without the beadhead, and then I remembered that it had been Lepage who had tied these and he would have the recipe, but I realized that if I went up to the house again to e-mail Jim I might never get back out here, where I had a book to finish that was already two weeks overdue. So I tied a dozen miniature beadhead caddis pupae that each looked radically different from the other and nothing at all like Lepage's original, and then I dribbled head cement on my watch while staring out the window with a bodkin poised in midair, and I noticed it was past five and then remembered it was Thursday and Linda was working and it was one of my days to cook supper, so I shut down the computer and headed for the house and found I'd forgotten to thaw the ducks the Post-it stuck to the freezer had promised for supper, so I scratched around and found some frozen leftover ham of uncertain vintage and six eggs and a mycologically active mill end of Gorgonzola and some spinach and scallions just poking toward eating size in the greenhouse, and I made omelets. I forget what happened after that.

The point of all this is that sometimes I don't do things the way other people do, not because I think I'm so clever I can figure out better ways to do everything or because I'm just contrary and I'm compelled to always cut against the grain—well, maybe a bit of that—but because sometimes my meager abilities aren't up to the task of doing something the proper way and I have to devise my own. And even when I'm physically or experientially up to a given task, all too often I'll nod thoughtfully and radiate comprehension throughout someone's patient explanation of an arcane and difficult process while I'm actually wondering whether it was my grandmother who kept lightbulbs in all the sockets because she was afraid electricity would leak out all over the floor, or if it was James Thurber's grandmother who kept lightbulbs in all the sockets because she was afraid electricity would leak out all over the floor and I'd just appropriated the memory.

But I digress.

Personally, I don't see anything at all eccentric about bass-bugging with a Spey rod. The best bass fisherman I ever knew didn't fish surface bugs, but he finessed big live shiners far back into distant lily pads, and he used a twenty-foot cane pole garnished with a handful of guides and a taped-on automatic fly reel, because, he'd said, "Long rod gimme *LAIGS*. I kin git places I cain't *GIT*."

I came to Spey rods while looking for a crutch, a way to get places I could no longer get. I had spent the first half of my life at hard, physical labor and never got so much as a hangnail, but six years of sitting at a desk and pecking daintily at a computer keyboard left me with a trendily fashionable ailment called carpal tunnel syndrome. Now, after six years of alternately immobilizing and refrigerating my extremities, gobbling painkillers, enduring sadistic physical therapy, and of course abandoning the high-pressure position with a harried little division of a Fortune 500 publisher that brought this on in the first place, I've grown as strong as an average six-year-old. Many things I once took for granted—like paddling a canoe all day or casting the length of a nine-weight line—have slipped permanently beyond my grasp, so to speak.

Which is particularly annoying when I think of how often I need to paddle a canoe all day or cast the length of a nine-weight line—whether to propel a big frog popper toward an unapproachable lily pad and its satellite porky largemouth or an even bigger saltwater popper toward a far-distant tide rip boiling with stripers the size of Poland Chinas.

But I have learned to adapt, hypochondriacally speaking. I take frequent meandering breaks from a workload intentionally kept undemanding. I have ergonomically revamped my workspace in the best information-age-casualty fashion. And I constantly monitor muscles and tendons for the chilling fingertips that say Back Off or spend a week in wrist splints. As I fish I try to avoid wind and, unfortunately for my casting, abrupt changes in velocity and direction. Lightweight trout rods fished at short distances bother me hardly at all these days, but with heavier rods I must limit both casting distance and time spent fishing, which of course limits my ability to fish. But there's an ergonomic adaptation available here, too.

New tools and innovative techniques emerge to fulfill specific requirements, and if ever there was a place where anglers needed a new tool and new techniques it was along Scotland's River Spey. In 1867 Francis Francis, longtime editor of *The Field*, described it in his classic *A Book on Angling* as a "magnificent river, which often gives grand sport; and as the river is large and the angling is mostly from the bank, and the banks are frequently high, while the stream is not only heavy but often tremendously rapid and rough as is the bottom, an indifferent fisherman cannot expect much sport on the Spey."

What evolved as a crutch for indifferent fishermen was less a new tool than a new way of using exaggerated versions of existing tools. These greenheart and Calcutta Spey rods were sixteen to twenty feet long and designed to be cast with two hands using a technique somewhere between an overhead cast—impossible on the Spey's steep banks—and a roll cast, which couldn't heave a heavy salmon fly far enough or accurately enough in the Spey's fast-running water to reach the salmon lies.

Think of a Spey cast as a change-of-direction roll cast made not from a stationary arc of line on the water, with the forward loop of line unrolling along the water's surface, but from a moving arc of line just briefly touching the water to your side and slightly behind you in a great Palmer-method *D*, with the forward-traveling loop unrolling entirely in the air. As Francis wrote, "This is not an easy cast to make, and requires a good deal of practice. It is hardly possible to describe it, and must be seen and studied to be understood clearly." Amen. But it *can* be done with a little study and practice, even by an East Tennesseean with no discernible attention span and all the brutish strength of a six-year-old. And it's worth the effort, for as European Atlantic salmon anglers have long known, with a two-handed rod you can fish a long line with heavy flies all day and live to tell about it, and you can do it, judging from some two-handed salmon anglers I've met, well into your dotage.

My Atlantic salmon trips are few and far between, but it's a poor technology that isn't transportable. As I played with my shiny new Spey rod and tried to figure out what Hugh Falkus was getting at in his Britannically eccentric book, *Spey Casting*, I began Walter Mittying visions of myself unfurling elegant Spey and two-handed overhead casts a hundred feet across the water with a mere flick of both wrists, only my visions didn't show me casting over classic sparkling salmon water but across tide rips and lily pads.

It's amazing what a modern fast-action Spey rod can do in experienced hands. At a fly-fishing show a few years ago I saw a scrawny Norwegian with an unpronounceable name and a two-handed fifteen-foot rod step up to the testosterone pit, where show-off mesomorphs were busily ripping out ninety-foot casts accompanied by all the requisite grunts, puffs, and shirt-ripping flexings of overdeveloped deltoids that make us normal people long for a loosening of justifiable-homicide laws. Hardly moving a muscle, he false-cast twice then fired 150 feet of line and backing right over the casting pool and straight out the door. The only sound you heard was the collective click of dropping jaws and the slither of something shriveling.

Judging from all the long rods I see sprouting from striper boats up and down the coast, the Spey rod is coming into its own on salt water. Indeed, Jim Vincent of RIO tells me some 30 percent of East Coast students in his popular Spey-casting seminars are salt-water anglers looking for an edge.

When something becomes popular I generally lose interest in it, but I like to think I have the eccentric niche of Spey-casting bass bugs all to myself. There's just something so deliciously peculiar about sculling along in a canoe through a malarial swamp, flippin' 'em ol' poppin' bugs at ol' Mistah Bucketmouth with a fifteen-foot fly rod designed to present princely Green Highlanders to the King of Fish.

When the leaden sophistication of contemporary trout fishing becomes overwhelming, it's generally to the bass world I retreat, wherein fun and whimsy are in the live well and kicking. To bass fishermen—at least those few who don't earn their living from it or aspire to—fishing is still simply a sport one does for fun and not a spiritual quest for self-realization.

After an evening's rise fraught with tongue-tangling entomological Latin, bass fishing is just so refreshingly and flamboyantly ungrammatical, like pilots became after Chuck Yeager convinced them having the Right Stuff meant stripping the *g* from every word that ever had one. Even high-Yankee bassmen from Minnesota and Michigan are always goin' bassin' or fishin'; I've never known one to go fishing or bassing, at least not in the pages of a bassin' magazine. Bass-fishin's apostrophication attained its apotheosis with a tubby crankbait called the Tennessee Kil'er. I can't figure out how to pronounce it and I was born and raised in Tenn'see.

Bass lures certainly sport more entertaining names than trout flies, perhaps because they look less like identifiable insects than like something one tries not to see in a truck-stop bathroom vending machine. Many imply something prurient sold furtively to people we hope don't live next door: Enticer, Undulator, Buzz Throb, Ripple Stick, Bang-Tail, Pork-O, Vibra Shaft, Hot Lips' Express. Some get wholesome down-home-on-the-farm names: BushHog, Timber Doodle, Woodchopper. Others threaten good-ol'-boy aggression: Assassinator, Aggravator, Kill'rB's, Evil Eel, Fatal Frog. Still others describe unsavory people—Meat Head, Husky

Jerk, Tailchaser, Psycho Path—or certain of their proclivities—
Mojo Reefer and Chug-N-Spit.

Fly-fishing names are far more refined, in a thin-lipped, humor-
less way: Light Cahill, Dark Hendrickson, Red Quill, March
Brown, Blue-Winged Olive, Pale Morning Dun—all entomologically correct and drearily dull. Perhaps it's grasping at straws to
imagine the Royal Humpy commemorates the Duke of Gloucester's brief reign.

Because they're considered less genteel than conventional trout
flies, streamers get gussied up with more suggestive names: Mickey
Finn, Streaker, Sucker Bait, Canadian Killer, Family Secret, Montreal Whore. It's hard to imagine a dry fly called the Beaverkill
Whore, although there is a Lady Beaverkill. We simply assume she
actually was.

A few weirdly named trout-specific dry flies are around—the
Tarantula and the Chernobyl Ant come to mind—but these are
aberrations, falling into the last-gasp grouping of what Charley
Waterman calls "something strange." Charley's theory is that "per-
ceptive trout, having become bored with their everyday diet however desirable it may be, sometimes prefer something a great deal
different." He described in a magazine article his unsuccessful
efforts to take trout from a fertile western spring creek carpeted
with tiny light cahills. He was matching the originals perfectly, he
said, but the fish weren't impressed, at least not until he tossed out
"a big, nameless fuzzy thing that looked like a bundle of trash from
under a fly tier's bench . . . and there was a big silent bulge by an
old log over against the bank 20 feet away" that rushed toward his
Something Strange, with the smaller trout parting reverentially to
let the monster pass by on its rendezvous with novelty.

I have long subscribed to the Something Strange theory when
faced with trout that refuse to behave as the books say they should,

or when hatch and fly downsize below my distance-vision abilities. My favorite Stranger, and the most successful dry fly I've ever used, is a size 8 or 10 Hornberg tarted up with a thick clump of pearl Flashabou presiding over a yellow marabou underwing. Seen from below, goes the theory, sunlight filtering through the mallard flank tent wing flashes all that 'bou softly and tenderly, like a tent-revival rent-a-sign beckoning the weary to come home.

Even though it looks ridiculously Brobdingnagian drifting through rafts of Lilliputian Paraleps, I've had big trout come halfway across a stream to take this fly, though I don't know whether they meant to eat it, defend their territory from it, or ask it for religious instruction.

The original Hornberg was a combination streamer-wet fly, and because my version is fished dry and differs in minor details from the original I've thought of giving it a nicely proprietary name. But too many folks are mildly modifying an old standard these days and claiming it as their own. Besides, Tennessee Kil'er is already taken.

I started this chapter looking for beadhead caddis pupae, and I don't have to tell you that beadhead pupae, nymphs, streamers, and Lord knows what else are all the rage these days. Beadheads have long gone from being a desperation-box gamble to a universal default choice. It's become almost impossible to find a fly fisher without a boxful of these lethal little jigs.

Jigs?

Call a subterranean fungus attractive to swine a truffle and you can sell it for a couple of hundred dollars a pound. Call a fly-rod jig a Beadhead Nymph, and Orvis will beat a path to your door.

The consensus is a weighted nymph is a fly, a beadhead nymph is a fly, even a lead-eyed Woolly Bugger is a fly—but a jig is a lure. And, goes the argument, real fly fishers don't fish with lures.

Years ago fly-rod lures were everywhere. Sporting magazines ran countless ads for tiny jigs, spoons, spinners, even a miniature Helin Flatfish—all designed specifically to be cast with a fly rod, and all attempts to impart the illusive quality of life to a tiny inanimate object.

Trout's brains are rudimentary, somewhere between a cockroach and a lizard, and although it's tempting to assign them a supernatural intelligence because they so frequently outwit highly evolved species like us, when feeding opportunistically and not keyed in to a specific hatch a trout's narrow-band synapses can process only a few simple computations. When an object floats into sight they want mostly to know Eat or Not Eat, to use the economical verbiage of Tonto, Tarzan, and Frankenstein. For a trout, distinguishing Eat from Not Eat is easy: Eat Move. Not Eat Not Move.

If we insist on catching trout by faking the living organisms on which they feed, our fakes should move, too. Even a dead-drift dry fly moves; its hackles flex in the current like the legs of a nervous mayfly; a deep-sunk nymph's rough-dubbed body and partridge hackle beard quiver seductively underwater like the gills and legs of a helpless drifting nymph. But nothing moves quite like a jig. As soon as tension on the line is released a jig's nose-heavy configuration sends it diving for the bottom, just like a larval fish or minnow that's spotted a predator and is heading for cover. With tension on the line a jig suspends horizontally in the water column like a minnow feeding on drift. Combine this natural behavior with a seductively waving hair or feather tail and a hook that always rides point-up and thus snag-free, and you have an almost foolproof lure—so effective that jigs are routinely part of abandon-ship kits in navies worldwide. If a jig won't catch fish, there aren't any fish.

Jig is a noun. Fished correctly it is also a verb. Back when I was lobstering I sometimes headed out to Matinicus Rock on Sundays to jig for cod with handlines and six-ounce chrome-plated diamond jigs. Up here in Maine that's called jerking for bottomfish—an apt description. Don Thomas, in an article about jigging for walleyes on the lower Missouri, wrote that "it's hard for me to get over its obvious resemblance to what used to be known as self-abuse: mindless, repetitive, up-and-down motions sustained by the conviction that gratification will eventually result if you keep it up long enough."

Bob Boyle, the fly-rod jig's most relentlessly enthusiastic proponent, tells me he manipulates his fly-rod jigs like an orchestra conductor wielding a baton. His favorite is the four-note opening to Beethoven's Fifth Symphony, meaning three grandiose four-inch rod-tip twitches and a one-foot pull: bum bum bum buuuuuuum. With different musical roots, and because I can mindlessly sing it all day, I favor the rhythm line to Bob Marley's "Crazy Baldhead": bop bop bop . . . boppa boppaaaaaaa. After a few minutes of that I'm bopping up the stream like, well, a Crazy Baldhead. The choice of music is yours, but you get the idea. To fish jigs you gotta have riddim, mon. And a thick skin, if morally superior anglers are nearby. Real fly fishers don't dance.

Fly-rod jigs are by definition mini jigs—sizes 8 through 18. And jigs are by definition simple: A puff of marabou or a pair of hackle tips for a tail, a slim fur, chenille, or herl body, and perhaps a sparse palmering of soft hackle. Color seems relatively unimportant, at least in the waters I've fished. I've found a tiny all-black jig with an ostrich herl body and a marabou tail effective on most freshwater species. Bob Boyle, who lives in an area with excessively educated trout, ties extremely realistic larval fish imitations by using strands of multicolored marabou for the tail and internal organs, then forming a body over that by molding to a fish shape (with wet fingers) semicured epoxy containing glitter. The effect perfectly duplicates the ethereal sparkling transparency of the naturals.

The shank of a proper purpose-built jig hook bends sharply up at right angles to the eye. These are available through size 10; below this you'll have to use standard down-eye hooks. Because fish often take jigs as they drift downward on a slack line, the hook points should be so sharp they frighten you.

For weight you can use brass or tungsten beads, but properly speaking a beadhead fly isn't really a jig because you can't position the weight in such a way that the hook point always rides up or adjust the balance by placing the weight directly beneath the eye. A true fly-rod jig is best weighted with a split shot (I use Dinsmore's Tin Shot, figuring even if lead isn't banned it should be), preferably pinched over a dab of Zap-A-Gap or Five-Minute epoxy. With a jig hook the weight is pretty much self-positioning; just pinch the split shot directly under the eye. With a standard down-eye hook you have to be more careful with placement. For the hook point to ride up, the split shot must be slightly biased toward the side of the shank opposite the point. Play around with different configurations in the bathtub until a dressed fly sinks at around a forty-five-degree angle, point-up.

Fly-rod jigs are a useful addition to the all-around fly fisher's bag of tricks. That some people will consider you less than a lady or gentleman for using them shouldn't dissuade you from trying them.

It might even be a reason.

11

Leave It to Beavers

Beavers are busy little fellows, beavers are.

—ANDY PANDA

*I*t used to be such a splendid little trout stream. Cold, freestone, never more than twenty-five feet wide, it cut quickly through a narrow wooded valley, plunging over sharp granite ledges, rushing across cobble riffles and drowned logs, spreading out across fine gravel tailouts then repeating the process at regular intervals for two isolated miles before easing into a deep pond impounded by a stonework dam that once powered a shipwright's sawmill.

Covering the little valley's steep sides were thick stands of spruce, hemlock, fir, striped maple, beech, yellow birch, and bigtooth aspen. Beneath the forest canopy, vestigial trails wandered through gaps in overgrown stone walls toward a cathedral of towering white pines, the last remnants of the hardscrabble farms that once covered the Maine countryside and of the great forest that sparred and planked the local fleet of China-trade square-riggers.

Transpiration from the thick evergreen canopy cooled the surrounding soil and its groundwater, which seeped endlessly into the stream through a thick sponge of intertwining roots. This, combined with a pair of strategically placed beaver dams, virtually eliminated the vicious cycle of flood and drought that scoured the life from less fortunate streams nearby.

Which is why this stream held a surprise: brook trout. *Big* brook trout. An experienced angler would look at that unremarkable water and figure it might hold an eight-incher or two, but over the years I caught and released a dozen better than twice that long and four that hit eighteen inches, and I know of at least three that nudged twenty inches and another that measured an even two feet, a hook-jawed, potbellied monster that fell to a neighbor's nightcrawler after three years' patient stalking.

That stream was an angler's paradise, one that, for a thousand or so feet, formed the western boundary of my backyard, the place where I expected to fish out my days in peace and plenty.

Then one day I heard chain saws.

They meant no harm, the pair of loggers I found busily at work. One was even an avid fly fisherman. But people have to make a living, and in these parts a lot of livings come from trees—cutting them, hauling them, making paper and studs and clothespins and toothpicks from them.

It's been that way since European settlers arrived here in the eighteenth century. Forests are cut down and forests regrow, an endless cycle. Done correctly there's nothing wrong with it, unless of course it's happening to forests that cool and filter and nourish a trout stream you hold dear.

The big pine grove went first, a heartrending ten-acre clear-cut. They high-graded the rest of the forty-acre lot, leaving behind little but immature or unmarketable weed trees.

To their credit, they ran their logging operation far better than the casually criminal approach of most peckerwood outfits. They tossed hay bales into gullies to reduce silt inflow, left a few large seed and den trees, and for the most part tried to skid logs across the slopes rather than up and down. But no matter how carefully operated, modern logging leaves permanent scars. Now—fifteen years after they bought that little parcel of land from the heirs of a defunct lumber company, fourteen years after they sold its skinned remains to retirees from away who imagined an investment opportunity, nine years after the retirees sold it to a pair of real estate developers blithely ignorant of wetlands protection laws, two weeks after the developers finally gave up and sold it to me for about the price of a new pickup truck—those skidder trails are still clawing away topsoil. Spongy hollows and springs that once metered out clear cool water year-round now jet topsoil soup when it's raining and bake hard as flue tiles when it isn't.

Tote roads cut out to the blacktop led in new people—fishermen, trail bikers, ATVers. This happens all the time, of course: Land gets sold, trees get cut, roads get built, new people come in. Another endless cycle, and one unlikely to end as long as we persist in reproducing and spreading ourselves ever farther into the last few remnants of wild.

But worse for that stream than the influx of motorized morons and thirty-trout-a-day scofflaws was a shortsighted beaver trapper, one who never read E. J. Dailey's 1940s classic *Traplines and Trails*, which cautions, "Never set traps for beaver when there is apparently only a pair of them living, for a catch will destroy a chance for greater rewards later on."

He needed only one winter to clean out the stream. The next season the upper beaver dam blew out, and water I'd fished right through August for ten years was gone—*gone*—by the second week of June. The following year the lower dam collapsed, and long stretches of deep holding water became thin sterile flats. Four times in fifteen years beavers tried to reoccupy the stream, only to be snared out each winter. Whole hatches of caddis, stoneflies, and mayflies disappeared, as did the in-stream tangle of blowdowns that sheltered and fed them. The trout disappeared, too, of course, at least the good ones.

Now when you look at that stream and figure an eight-incher would be a good fish, you'd be right.

And when I look at that stream, the new owner of just under a mile of frontage on one bank and a quarter mile on both, the de facto steward of a watershed, I see both opportunities and responsibilities. And one helluva lot of work.

A good trout stream needs a steady flow of well-oxygenated cold water, spawning gravel, a food base, and some kind of cover—boulders, downed trees, root wads, overhanging banks. Streams that have these features produce trout; streams that don't, don't, at least not in entertaining quantities. Once a watershed is made healthy by reducing erosion—revegetating slopes, filling gullies with brush, excluding livestock, trail bikes, and other vermin—modern stream improvement follows with various forms of artificially constructed trout cover along with minimalist dams designed to slow and redirect water flow.

Studying the abundant literature of trout-stream improvement brings excitement at the possibilities and a new vocabulary, including cool words like *thalweg*, which sounds like a swordsman from *Beowulf* but is actually a line between a section of a streambed's highest and lowest points. But that abundant literature also brings a growing apprehension about the sheer labor involved in improving nature. The books are plump with discouraging photographs showing heavy equipment engaged in drastic riparian sculpting, along with teams of grunting mesomorphs heaving into place pre-fabricated timber trout hotels and K-dams and pinning them to the streambed by pounding in concrete reinforcing bars.

I look at my narrow wooded valley and wonder what it costs to lower a backhoe by helicopter, and at my hard granite streambed and wonder where I'll find a portable pile driver for the rebar, or a muscular work crew that won't expect to be paid handsomely or, worse, to have perpetual fishing rights—all this assuming, of course, that an indifferent government functionary actually grants permission to alter a flowing stream, even if those alterations merely restore, in an artificial sense, what once was there.

But there's an obvious way around all this governmental per-mitting and the sobering expense of aerial machinery insertion and hired labor, and it avoids the need to slaughter volunteer workers to ensure their silence. It is, of course, the beaver. Beavers don't need official sanction to cut a streamside tree or erect an unobtrusive dam, they provide both initial construction and per-petual maintenance services for free, and they don't tell their friends about this great little spot they know about.

Virtually extinct in eastern North America at the turn of the century, beaver populations are now growing rapidly across the country, so much so that "problem beavers," meaning those that look at a low-lying roadway or golf course and envision a pond, have become an epidemic. Because landowners willing to resettle delinquent beavers are few and far between, many end up trapped and killed. Which is why I've decided to become a modern-day Father Flanagan and open, on my little trout stream, a resettlement shelter protected by a no-trapping ban from the pen of a sympathetic state wildlife biologist, a Beavers Town, to draw parallel imagery from the 1938 movie about a sheltering haven for wayward boys. Although I look less like Spencer Tracy than like a cross between Elmer Fudd and Pee-wee Herman, I am definitely getting into the role. Surely my self-congratulatory glow has nothing to do with the possibility of finding two-foot wild brook trout sixty seconds from my office—all at no cost to my pocketbook, back, or privacy.

Beavers and brook trout came out of the Pleistocene as closely connected as Nureyev and Fonteyn or Ward and June Cleaver. I doubt brook trout did much for beavers beyond reducing the numbers of mosquitoes and blackflies that swarm whenever pensive beaver heads surface, but beavers certainly benefited brook trout, turning endless miles of marginal trout habitat into brook trout nirvana. Although beavers can absolutely destroy trout fishing in low-gradient streams with borderline temperatures, such as are common in Wisconsin or Michigan, on high-gradient streams in colder regions like Wyoming and Maine it's quite a different story. Beaver ponds moderate seasonal oscillations in water levels, minimizing both floods and droughts; they trap sediment and filter water, impound deep pools for a freeze-free refuge, and increase in-stream woody debris, providing cover for fish and forage for invertebrates. It's a marriage made in heaven, or at least in the last ice age, and one that directly benefits trout fishers and other worthy wetland denizens such as amphibians and waterfowl.

Like most backcountry trout fetishists, I spend a great deal of time searching out tiny streams sporting new beaver ponds, which within a year or two can turn an otherwise lackluster trout trickle into the finest kind of angler's amusement park. Understandably, the location of new ponds is a secret guarded as closely as the formula for Coca-Cola.

The first few weeks after ice-out, when it's still too cold to fish in an interesting fashion, are the best times to search for beaver ponds. Armed with an educated guess gleaned from topographic maps—you need no more exotic logic than thinking, Where would I build a pond if I were a beaver?—you cruise backroads culverts looking for freshly chewed sticks brought down on the spring rise, then search carefully upstream.

I say carefully because fishing beaver ponds can be dangerous, especially when dams are new and therefore unstable. Just the thought of walking across a new beaver dam made of loosely inter-woven sharpened sticks conjures images of corn dogs and Vlad the Impaler. But an even better argument for staying off the dam is rooted less in minimizing self-perforation than in maximizing the chance at a big fish: A beaver pond's hot spots are immediately below the dam, where the overflow scours out a hole, and imme-diately above the spillway, which is generally the deepest part of the pond and eventually channels by most of the drifting food. A sloppy approach is flat-out guaranteed to put down those big fish. Other hot spots are near the entrance to the lodge, which can be either the familiar wattle-and-daub dome or an inconspicuous bankside burrow (like the lair of the two-footer my neighbor caught); near the tangled mass of submerged sticks that serves as a winter food supply; and along the deep bottom trenches beavers dredge to ensure wintertime navigation.

Carefully pretty much describes everything you need to know about fishing a beaver pond, for the water is usually crystal clear, cover is hard to find, and the acoustic properties of the mud-and-tussock shoreline transmit your presence to suspicious lateral lines faster than you can say oops. If I'm fishing up a small stream with my standard seven-foot 4X leader and see a beaver pond around the bend, I'll change down to longer and finer—maybe twelve feet of 6X, and sometimes better—and approach the pond like a bow hunter stalking deer. Even then I'm rewarded more often by the sight of a big swirling tail than by the pull of a good fish on the line, but then fly fishing is supposed to be full of difficult uncertainties; otherwise it would not hold an intelligent person's interest.

John Gierach wrote in his first book, *Fly Fishing Small Streams*, that "without beaver ponds, some little streams would be useless to all but the craziest of fly fishermen." To which I add that, with a little time and a suspension of trapping until a self-sustaining beaver population emerges and a strictly regulated trapping season thereafter, those of us lucky enough to own a bit of trout stream can dramatically improve the fishing without damaging our reputations as the laziest of fly fishermen.

I'm still waiting for the fishing to dramatically improve on my insignificant little stream, but I suspect I won't be waiting too long: Yesterday morning I found naked gnawed stumps where a matched pair of black ash once towered over the stream, and when I slipped back late in the evening and tripped over a log in the dark, I heard the most satisfying sound a freestone fly fisher can hear: the liquid *kerwhack* of a delinquent beaver pulling the alarm, a brief interruption in the eternal busyness of living out a long and purposeful life.

12

Gone Mad in the Midday Sun

Though related to a peer,
I can hand, reef, and steer,
And ship a selvagee;
I am never known to quail
At the fury of a gale,
And I'm never, never sick at sea!

—SIR WILLIAM GILBERT,
HMS Pinafore

"Never," it says in a book called *Successful Shark Fishing*. "Never bring a live shark into a boat." Yet not only is a very pissed-off eighty-pound blue shark most definitely in this boat, but the author of that book, A. J. Campbell, is holding it up like a wet dog and grinning like a ninny, I'm firing my camera like a madman, and from far aloft in the tuna tower comes the screech of hysterical laughter: Our captain has been treed. We're in the Gulf of Maine

125

fly fishing for blue sharks—blue doggies, as the dragger boys say. It's a busman's holiday at the end of a busy season of guiding for A. J. and editing one too many books for me, a trip undertaken by captain and crew and freeloading guest purely for pleasure, not profit. The day started out autumnally Maine—gray, gusty, and cold—but a few miles back we emerged from the fog into an alien landscape of slick-calm seas lit by a burning sun. It looks less like late-September Maine than the plains of India, and for weirdly associative reasons we find ourselves singing English showtunes.

Back in the 1970s Rip Cunningham caught the first blue shark on a fly in the Gulf of Maine. Shortly afterward A. J. Campbell caught the second, and he's been at it ever since, guiding scores of anglers looking to take a truly large fish on a fly for a lot less money than an offshore billfish trip to Ecuador or Hawaii. We're on Captain Ken Sullivan's Blackfin 36, *Hopscotch II,* one of a handful of charter boats specializing in offshore fly-fishing trips for sharks, tuna, and what few other large Gulf of Maine species the commercial fishermen haven't vacuumed up in a last-gasp effort to make their boat payments.

The Gulf of Maine may well have the world's best fishing for blue sharks, due in part to all those commercial fishermen. Every day bottom draggers haul aboard the sweepings of their ruinous ravaging tows and cull through tons of wriggling fish looking for a handful of legally marketable sizes and species; the vast piles of rejects get unceremoniously shoveled over the side, where the faithful blue doggies wait openmouthed, fulfilling their end of a one-sided bargain that has existed as long as humans have fished.

In the olden days blue sharks were called blue whalers, from their habit of relentlessly following whaling ships and gnawing hunks from carcasses during cutting in—not to mention snarfing up any hapless hands who might slide off a greasy wallowing whale. Not surprisingly, commercial seamen hated blue sharks then and they hate them still: Blues wreck gear, fishermen will tell you; they eat fish off trawl lines and chew them out of gill nets. And unlike the valuable mako, which tastes enough like swordfish for unscrupulous fish dealers to slide it by patrons as routinely as they do ten-dollar sea scallops cookie-cuttered from two-dollar skate wings, blue doggies are commercially valueless, their taste most often compared with a piss-soaked sponge.

Of course sport fishermen, especially northeastern sport fishermen, judge value on a different scale, on which blue sharks rank very near the top. Ranging between fifty and three hundred pounds, blues are ideal quarries for light-tackle anglers and fly rodders: better fighters and more accessible than the deep-dwelling porbeagles that also frequent these waters, and both more plentiful and more manageable than their distant relatives the makos. True, the mako is one of the world's great gamefish, but to me, being connected via fly line to a half-ton fish that can jump ten feet high and land in the boat with its appetite intact doesn't really qualify as amusement.

After an hour or so of running and trading lines from *H.M.S. Pinafore* we hit A. J.'s favorite shark hole, an ephemeral GPS spot suspended over some five hundred feet of green sea halfway between the Harris Ground and The Kettles, two groundfishing sites about twenty miles south of Boothbay Harbor, Maine, that have been fished since the sixteenth century. A. J. gets on the VHF and hails the *Kayla D.*, a twenty-nine-footer out of Bath hull-down on the horizon. They've been here a few hours, fishing live mackerel on light stand-up rods with twelve-pound tippets and looking for a light-tackle record. Captain Dave Dooley reports a half-dozen sharks around them, one a thirteen-footer he said would go three hundred pounds easily. Too much fish for our fly rods, A. J. says. He's using a burly thirteen-weight boron number of his own design, and I've got a prototype nine-weight that Orvis unwisely loaned me for testing, probably thinking I had stripers and bluefish in mind. Hey, testing is testing.

A. J. unmolds a frozen bucket of ground pogies into a mesh bag protected by a plastic milk crate and tosses it over the side. A light line tethers this chum dispenser to the stern; when we hook up we'll cast it off, where it'll bob in our wake, supported by an orange-bubble mooring float and continuing to squoosh out eau de pogie while we're off fighting the fish.

Shark fishing feels very unlike any other fishing. That a shark is the only gamefish that might eat you imparts a subliminal edge of hormonal bravado to the already weird atmosphere, and everything we do seems funnier than it really is. Of course we're in no real danger in a stout thirty-six-foot sportfisherman like this, but it's hard to forget that hunter and hunted can change roles quickly off soundings, where you never know what'll come sniffing up a chum slick or what kind of mood it'll be in. Not long ago one of A. J.'s sports hooked into a twelve-hundred-pound mako near here that casually peeled off six hundred yards of line without ever realizing it was hooked. And on a scalloping trip just to the north a few years back, I saw a great white cruising the surface that looked longer than our boat.

Despite all the shark-alarm-saturated media, sharks have suffered far more over the years from human actions than we have suffered from theirs. After the movie *Jaws*, millions of sharks died worldwide to assuage primitive male urges more commonly quelled by the purchase of a red Corvette. Thousands more die every year as commercial by-catch or as targeted species tossed back alive, their soupfins hacked away with hatchets. Although sharks swam these seas a hundred million years before dinosaurs walked the earth, today many populations are in danger. Sharks are not prolific breeders and take a long time to reach sexual maturity. Sport fishers who don't fancy freezing a half ton of uremic shark meat should let them go. Carefully. A photograph of a manly male mugging in front of a sagging gape-mouthed shark carcass doesn't say Brave Angler. It says Small Penis.

Forty-five minutes after throwing over the chum ball the first blue weaves slowly into view, a seven-footer that A. J. estimates at eighty pounds. The burning sun and unruffled surface and whiffs of rotting pogies that are turning us into modern major generals gone mad—and slightly green around the gills—in the midday sun make her wary, suspicious of the red-and-orange tarpon fly A. J. twitches slowly past her nose. After a dozen bobbing and weaving passes she finally turns and snaps at it, A. J. leans back on the rod, the reel begins to squall, Ken cranks an engine, and we're off. The trick in taking sharks on light tackle is to keep them from rolling up in the line, best done by angling the boat so the line pulls always from the shark's side, never from astern. Theoretically you can land them without following in the boat. Theoretically. But given time, a shark's sandpaper skin can saw through even a wire bite tippet; a monofilament leader won't last half a minute if the shark turns tail and runs. And it will.

After several good runs on the surface and a lot of thrashing the blue is alongside and the real fun begins. A. J.'s friend Barry Gibson, editor of *Saltwater Sportsman,* dared him to bring a blue into the boat for a photograph. Under the glare of the midday sun and the fog of pogie fumes this seems like a fine idea. I lean over and grab the leader above the shark's mouth while A. J. fumbles a rope around its tail, hoists it aboard, and holds it up for the camera. It's all over in a couple of minutes, and it's only then that we realize how hormonally asinine we've been. And how much fun it was.

Now back to the chum ball and it's my turn. By now four or five sharks are butting and rubbing against the milk crate like cats around catnip, including one big boy around nine feet long—too much for my borrowed nine-weight. I cast a 4/0 blue-and-green Deceiver to a six-footer that will probably go around sixty-five pounds, but he wants nothing to do with it—won't even look at it, in fact. Again I quote from A. J.'s book. Navy tests, I remind him, proved that sharks are most attracted to—surprise—International Orange, the color of life vests. On goes an orange tarpon fly and in two twitches I'm hooked up.

The fight is short and technical: The boat keeps abreast of the fish, I keep applying sideways pressure, the blue runs twice, and I let him go then pump him back. Within fifteen minutes—the magic angling threshold between fun and work—he's boatside. A. J. reaches over and pulls the fly loose, and the largest fish I've taken on a fly noses back down into the depths.

Now it's Captain Ken's turn. Ken has fished conventional tackle for years, but today he'll try to take his first shark on a fly, and he'd like to make it a good one. Right on cue the nine-footer ghosts from beneath the boat, scattering the pack of six- and seven-footers swirling around the chum ball. Ken twitches the red-and-orange streamer by the big shark. At first he ignores it and heads back beneath the boat, but then he turns violently and takes the fly in a swirl. The thirteen-weight bows double, A. J. cranks up an engine, and we're off to the races. Even with the big rod Ken has all he can handle. After twenty minutes it's apparent that he's positively suffering. It's also apparent, from his TV-fishing-show whoops and hollers, that he's having almost too much fun. We all are. Finally the big shark is boatside, A. J. cuts the leader, and we sit down to eat lunch and watch the terns, gulls, and gannets skim the sea for bits of chum.

We're arguing the identity of what we finally agree is a northern fulmar paddling slowly up the chum slick when a fast-moving hump of water behind it sprouts a pair of fins like a *Los Angeles*-class attack sub charging to the surface in a navy recruitment ad, and the fulmar leaps into the air just inches ahead of a big shark's straining jaws. And now the sea begins to boil with sharks chasing birds—a would-be feeding frenzy—and to fly fishermen gone mad in the midday sun it's something more: a hatch, or at least a spinner fall. We are consumed by the idea of taking a shark on a dry fly.

A. J. produces a giant orange deer hair bug with teddy-bear eyes and a long, saddle hackle tail—the closest thing to a bird we have on board. I cast it into the thick of the fray, pop it twice across the surface, and the ocean yawns open. Try to imagine an eighty-pound largemouth hitting a popper ten feet from your face, only give it a mouthful of teeth and backdrop it with scenes from B-movies, Discovery Channel documentaries, and odd bits of Gilbert and Sullivan.

This fish is about twenty pounds heavier than my first, and the nine-weight is taxed to its limits. After fifteen minutes of slugging it out I finally maneuver the big blue boatside, where she lies motionless. From her mouth dangles a moss-covered hook and a length of thick twine, a souvenir from one of the murderous long-lines that indiscriminately slaughter sharks and billfish worldwide. As we lean over the side with Nikons clacking away, the shark comes to life, thrashing wildly and soaking the paparazzi, then heads straight for the bottom. In less than two minutes she bulls off 250 yards of backing; only about three wraps remain on the spool before she stops and I face a long, slow slog to the surface.

The loaner's backbone proves up to the task, but mine is wearing out fast. After half an hour of tedious pumping the fly line finally comes into view; only ninety more feet to go. Then the rod begins to throb and jerk—the shark is wrapping herself up in the line and there's nothing I can do about it. Five minutes later it goes limp and I reel in. The leader is worn through and the first twenty feet of fly line look like they've been eaten by a disk sander.

What the hell. We've all caught fish, it's getting dark, the chum has lost its savor if not its odor, and we decide to head for home. By now we've finally stopped singing Gilbert and Sullivan, but it'll be hours before we stop laughing.

13

Thy Rod and Thy Staff

His fishing was not a sport, nor solely a means of subsistence, but a sort of solemn sacrament and withdrawal from the world, just as the aged read their Bibles.

—HENRY DAVID THOREAU, *A Week on the Concord and Merrimack Rivers*

Morning on the Miramichi. At the head of the pool, two frail old men wade waist-deep into the swift river, palsied hands clasping stout wooden sticks. Three casts, then three slow but sure steps downstream, shorn up by their staffs like Old Testament patriarchs.

Afternoon on the South Platte. Ben feels his way slowly into the current, leaning on a folding staff and picking trout from pockets that I—taller, younger, a more experienced wader, presenting less surface area to the hydraulic rush—have tried to reach and cannot.

133

Evening on the Penobscot. I slip and slide atop the greased car-ronade shot that passes for bottom here, watching dainty Hendrick-sons squirt to the surface and hoping to reach casting position without putting down this smooth hushed pool filled with feeding salmon. *Kawhap.* With a great beavertail slap I'm facedown and struggling, and the splashy rises that mean small salmon and the tiny O-rings that mean large ones vanish with the last gray twi-light. As the Hendricksons continue to pop off, I slosh ashore to build a fire and fume.

The knees go first followed closely by nerve, or so former dancers and football players tell me. It's the same with anglers, or at least it is with those of us who wade. Only last season, it seems, I was a hip-booted Baryshnikov leaping from rock to rock and towing a roostertail wake across deep churning runs. But in truth I had been slowing down for years: compensating, ignoring, denying, like all the elderly teenagers of my generation, the undeniable fact that aging forces, as Jung wrote, a contraction of life.

My own contraction became undeniable a couple of years ago when I drove a few hours north to revisit a fierce and secret mountain stream I had fished every weekend for seven years, until combat logging killed both its fishing and its splendid isolation. Now, twenty years after the logging crews left for greener fields, the stream and its little valley had begun to heal. The towering hemlock and pine were gone, but young spruce and striped maple softened the steep banks, and the broad wet platters of moose tracks glistened in marsh grass scabbing over the bleeding scars of skidder trails.

Up past the third bend and the half mile of sterile, shallow flats that hid this best of all small streams from unadventurous anglers, things were much as I'd left them. The ghost of my old trail still sidled down to the granite ledge where I had begun so many splendid days. A fat wild brookie rose to my Adams from the off-current curl where one had always risen, and the piano-size boulders stair-stepped up the mountainside as they always had, inviting one to hopscotch back and forth across a narrow channel too deep and swift and featureless to wade. The boulder trail led some seven miles upstream, to a sheer falls and a meandering moose path that wound back to the tote road and my hidden truck, to which I had returned tired and happy on countless days, rarely having wet more than my ankles and spending, or so it seems, as much time in the air as on the rocks.

I released that first trout and prepared to jump eight feet to the next boulder, as I had a hundred times and more, but now it seemed so far. What if I missed and twisted a knee? Broke a leg? An arm? A skull? A fly rod?

I picked my way along the steep bank, feeling for footholds, hanging from roots, trying to cross, looking for a way to reenter the network of launching and landing pads that had once made trout fishing here an acrobatic ballet. But before a mile had passed I gave up and drove home, traveling quickly and irrevocably away from carefree youth and into timid middle age.

Not so very long ago I made fun of wading anglers poking along with their staffs. It's Handicap Night, I'd say to my dim-bulb friends; hand me down my walkin' cane, har har har. Well, times have changed: As I watched others go where I no longer could, it became apparent that to fish on through my waning thirty years as I had fished during my first forty, I too needed something I could lean on.

Of course humans have been leaning on staffs as long as we have been humans. They were our first tools, our first weapons, our indispensable companions for eons, or so history tells us. A dying Jacob leaned on a staff and blessed his sons. Moses held a staff as he led the children of Israel out of Egypt. Charlton Heston held a staff as he led a thousand extras across the sands of a Paramount backlot. The alleged Little John beat the hubris out of the alleged Robin Hood with a staff and so sealed a legendary friendship. More recently, backpacking guru Colin Fletcher wrote in *The Complete Walker* that he takes his staff along almost as automatically as he takes his pack. "It is a third leg to me—and much more besides ... it converts me when I am heavily laden from an insecure biped into a confident tripod."

Modern-day anglers seem always heavily laden, and the average trout stream affords footing far less secure than most hiking trails. Thus fly fishers are consummate candidates to evolve into tripodal beings, and we needn't wait for a midlife crisis before growing a new appendage.

The best-known third leg of an angler's tripod is the Folstaf, whose six flare-fitted aluminum sections collapse down to a very pocketable nine inches. When conditions warrant or nerves fail, this compact bundle is drawn from its scabbard and, thanks to internal shock-cording, leaps forth like Excalibur into a sturdy fifty-two-inch staff, on the business end of which is a hardened steel point and on the other a comfortable cork handle topped with a tripod screw for your camera.

A couple of other collapsible staffs are available, and although I've not tried them extensively, it's likely they're cut from roughly the same aluminum tubing as the Folstaf and the similar (though sturdier, with nonjamming shouldered ferrules and a slightly less compact put-up) Cascade Designs Fish Stick, imitation being, well, you know. I would avoid staffs that extend using twist-lock cams, however; I've yet to find one that doesn't ooze shut under pressure at stupendously inconvenient times.

As undeniably convenient as the collapsible staffs are, they are difficult to love. Cold and unyielding, they sink to the bottom at the end of their tethers and tangle in your feet as you turn to move, and their metallic tap-tap-tapping sounds like Blind Pew searching out the Admiral Benbow to slip someone the black spot. Given the physics of underwater sound travel, this just has to scare hell out of the trout.

Although I carry a folding staff when I travel, for everyday wading I've come to prefer something fixed, buoyant, organic. In other words, a stick. But not just any stick.

You'll rarely see an old-timer from the southern Appalachians afield without his stout hickory staff. Not only does it help him cover the miles and negotiate the wild terrain, but it also clears away spiderwebs from trails, knocks water from overhanging leaves, fends off snakes and even, from time to time, bears and wild hogs.

In Maine, canoe poles are as common as paddles; some folks favor white ash, but the cognoscenti prefer black spruce, the knottier the better, as this reduces the risk of splitting. Hickory, ash, spruce, apple, maple—all make decent wading staffs. A wood staff is silent and resilient, and when tethered with twine it floats out of the way downstream as you fish. Unless shod with a collar of soft iron or aluminum, the tips eventually mushroom and wear away, but as is the case with aluminum staffs, a shod staff's tapping quickly telegraphs your unwelcome presence.

Fortunately there is a perfect material for wading staffs, and it carries the very appropriate name of ironwood. Both the hop hornbeam *(Ostrya virginiana)* and the hornbeam *(Carpinus caroliniana)* are generically called ironwood, but I'd trust my life only to *Carpinus,* and it's not easy to find. Look in fertile bottomlands for a slim trunk rippled like a power lifter's forearm and clad in smooth gray bark. The buds are squarish, brown, and angled, the leaves birchlike and symmetrical. Because it's so hard to work with tools, you'll want to find a sapling that when peeled is just the right diameter—an inch and a half or so. Grub around in the soil at the tree's base and you may find a crooked section of root that forms a natural handle.

I say all this in theory, because I'm still looking for the right iron-wood sapling and making do in the interim with a length of lumberyard ash closet pole. But I know what to look for and where to look, because for one brief day I owned the perfect wading staff.

As usual, Tom and Will and I took convoluted paths into our secret spot on the West Branch. We had never seen anyone there we had not brought with us, but today someone had been there. A crumpled hat sat on a rock, and nearby lay a wooden wading staff. We speculated about the owner's fate, wondering if he'd lost them upstream and they had fetched up here, wondering if he'd set his staff aside for a moment, slipped on the grease-ball rocks, and gone feet-first through the chute to become yet another cross on the banks of this wild river, so much more dangerous than it looks—and it *looks* dangerous.

Then a good fish rose and we lost interest in his fate, and because my Folstaf's tap-tap-tapping had driven me nuts all day I folded it away, picked up the wooden staff, and headed for the tailout. As the evening floated along the staff seemed to grow to my hand, or I seemed to grow to the staff. It was burnished white and gnarled with an unsplittable tangle of interlocking grain, its handle a smoothly swelling knob shielded by a half circle of natural crook. Below the handle a six-inch section of French-hitched seine twine stopped with a Turk's head at each end formed an elegant and slip-proof vertical grip, and below this a neatly chamfered hole held a lanyard of quarter-inch nylon back-spliced onto a stainless-steel halyard snap and swivel. Clearly this had been a cherished tool, crafted by someone who knew the old ways of the sea.

I took it back to camp and fished with it all the next day, easing into places I had not been in years. That evening we returned to our hole to see what it held. As night drew near and I tied on a tiny caddis emerger for the nightly hatch, a head popped from the puckerbrush behind, an elderly man as surprised to see me as I was to see him.

"I never seen nobody fish here before," he said, shaking his head. "I thought I was the only body that knew about this place."

"So did we," I said. "We've been here a while; want to take a turn?"

"No, go ahead," he said, introducing himself as Ray, a retired lobsterman from Portland. "I'll go up here and fish those two rocks; that's where I always fish."

As he began to hobble upriver using a rough pole of unpeeled maple, I picked up my spiffy new staff and turned toward the tailout, and it caught Ray's eye.

"Where'd ya get that staff?" he said.

"Found it here on the bank last night. Corker, ain't it?"

"Would ya believe me if I said it was mine?"

I handed it over, regret written all over me, and we sat down to chat.

"It's ironwood," Ray said. "Found it in a beaver dam. That's the best place to find these. The beavers strip the bark and tuck it into the dam, ya see, and the wood seasons real slow, the way it ought to. That way it don't split. Hard as iron. Had a helluva time boring that hole. Had to use a drill press. I've had it nearly fifteen years and the tip's still not worn down. It's got me out of more trouble than I can remember. Glad ya found it. Didn't want to face fishing out what's left of my life without that stick."

His sharp blue eyes twinkled beneath wild white eyebrows, a wise little Gandalf of the Penobscot.

"Ya get my age, wife gone and all, no kids, ya don't have that much to look forward to 'cept for this right here," he said, holding up a worn old F. E. Thomas and sweeping the tip of his staff up and down the darkening river. "But my rod and my staff, here. Well hell, you know. They comfort me."

And we sat there together on the bank, Ray and me, watching the sun sink into the river and waiting for time to bring us, among other less urgent things, a caddis hatch.

Branching Out

Travel is fatal to prejudice, bigotry, and narrow-mindedness, and many of our people need it sorely on these accounts. Broad, wholesome, charitable views of men and things cannot be acquired by vegetating in one little corner of the earth all one's lifetime.

—MARK TWAIN, *The Innocents Abroad*

I'm not fond of traveling—spending indeterminate hours aboard a flying subway sandwiched between Flatulent Grampy and Nervous Mommy and her Colicky Baby while wondering if the pilot is happy at home, and then fidgeting in an endless immigration queue and worrying about lost luggage and whether I fit the customs profile for cavity searches.

But I enjoy interesting food and interesting people and interesting scenery and interesting fishing, and if I argue the parochial view that I have more of all these within an hour of my house than I could ever hope to enjoy in my remaining ambulatory years, I could equally argue from an editor's view that professional fish-writers who write only of their own backyards and specific interests must have either enormous backyards and wide-flung interests or some other means of earning a living.

By this I mean that travel writing and modern fish-writing have become inexorably intertwined, bound together by vast numbers of avid fly fishers who, for reasons that elude me but which make perfect sense to them, live where there is no fishing, and by the equally vast numbers of fly-fishing outfitters beckoning them to luxurious lodges flung wide across the planet. And of course all those outfitters want to be glowingly featured in glossy fishing magazines in hopes of convincing the fishing-deprived that only a phone call to the outfitter's reservation desk and a valid credit-card number can save them from a slough of despond.

That I'm both an uncomfortable observer of and a willing participant in the global industrialization of fly fishing I excuse by declaring myself a Gemini, which, as I was told some years ago by a young woman who sought absolution in star charts and face painting for the sin of majoring in marketing, means two persons in one. And although as a diviner of the future I rate astrology only slightly more effective than goat entrails, I do find the characteristics of My Sign, as astrological initiates and singles-bar habitués say, provide convenient cover for these and other usefully contradictory viewpoints.

Corporeally speaking, I've taken a few good trips to exotic angling locales and, I hope, written about them without sliding into the mercantile murk of infomercial-land. And I've taken a few bad trips, too, where the outfitter's rosy advance billing conflicted with grim reality. In these cases I followed my mother's advice not to write anything at all if I could not write something nice.

On the whole, however, I've found fly-fishing outfitters, though their ranks be surprisingly rife with ex-marketing majors, to be an honest and accommodating lot. But there was this one trip . . . I call it Bob and Ted's Excellent Adventure, Bob and Ted having been two participants and it having been an adventure; the Excellent is meant to be ironic.

It seems this urban fly-shop owner owed my rod-maker friend Bob for an inventory of fly rods, and by way of sidestepping the issue and hopefully gaining some business advantages he offered Bob a salmon-fishing trip to his new lodge on the famous Miramichi River, providing Bob would in turn invite a couple of his fish-writer friends, meaning Ted and Me, in hopes one or both of us would write a story that would generate business.

This sounded okay to me—writing about lodges and such is part of my job, after all, and the three of us, flung out across the continent as we are, don't get to fish together that often. So I gave Our Host, who in the interests of avoiding unpleasant entanglements with libel lawyers I'll call Larry, the same assurances I always give in these situations: I'll write about your lodge if it proves to be the kind of place I think readers might want to go, and I'll write about it in a way that in some fashion amuses me and, hopefully, the readers, though there's a chance it may not amuse you. I'll pay my travel expenses and the guide's gratuity (as is customary for this sort of thing), and you'll pick up all the rest of the expenses. I always say this with ponderous self-importance, hoping to imply rock-ribbed old-money integrity but probably sounding like an aluminum-siding salesman. But then we all must have our delusions. Especially Geminis, or so I'm told.

So Ted flew in from Oregon, and Bob picked him up at the Boston airport and headed for Maine, and the next day we drove to the Miramichi, stopping in Doaktown to buy flies and soak up some authentic Atlantic salmon mystique, this being Bob and Ted's first trip ever for the King of Fish and my first trip since I'd stopped by a noted salmon pool on the Machias River many years ago and spotted three salmon, and I said to the Fish & Game biologist scribbling in his notebook nearby that it looked like a good season, and he said He guessed it wasn't, since he'd been monitoring the river all year and as far as he knew those were the only three salmon that had been anywhere near it, and I became depressed and starting muttering about great auks and passenger pigeons and went bass fishing instead.

We drove by famous lodges and famous pools with names you'd recognize if I wasn't afraid the libel lawyers would recognize them, too, and finally we found the place, a newish log cabin right on the banks of the storied Miramichi. Larry and his friend welcomed us warmly, and we ate royally and talked about the great fishing he'd had last year and about his plans for his new lodge and the high-roller clientele he hoped to attract—drawn here, he hinted, by the glowing account of our experiences he hoped to see soon in our respective magazines.

After supper I noticed the river looked different, as though it had somehow lost elevation, and I wandered down and discovered the river *was* different, for the tide had gone out.

"Larry," I said. "Salmon don't hit flies in salt water."

"Right," he said. "But I've got two of the best guides on the river working for me, and they'll be along tomorrow morning to take you to the best fishing on the Miramichi."

So the next morning the guides showed up and introduced themselves, then they led us to the public water in town open to anyone with a fishing license and a five-dollar bill for parking at the head guide's aunt's house, and we got in the rotation line and fished repeatedly and unsuccessfully down through the fifty yards of theoretical holding water while our guides lounged in lawn chairs and solicitously offered us sips of springwater from imperfectly cleansed plastic milk jugs.

Then that night it came on to rain, biblically speaking, and it kept at it all the next day, through which we fished in the other guide's aunt's backyard and in a nearby tributary, also unsuccessfully. And it rained all that night and into the next day.

I don't hold this against Larry, of course. It always rains when I go fishing, or the wind blows, or it both rains and blows. I seldom read about this in travel articles by other fish-writers, who, it seems, are eternally blessed with lovely weather and chirping birds and cooperative fish. Aldo Leopold wrote that books about nature seldom mention wind because they are written behind stoves. I can't speak for other fish-writers, but I usually write very near a stove and am always mentioning wind, though this may be mere whining on my part. I understand that's a Gemini trait as well.

We fished unsuccessfully through the morning, but after lunch I finally drew blood: two tiny terrified brook trout clinging to my big Butterfly for protection from the raging flood. Shortly afterward I landed the stern half of a red fox—a male, alas, and of no use for Hendrickson dubbing; then I hooked a fifteen-foot black spruce with six feet of bank attached; I followed it down the bank for a hundred feet, but it broke me off going over a falls and I had to watch helplessly as it swirled downriver toward its rendezvous with the sea. By way of congratulation, one guide eased forward from his lawn chair and offered a sip of springwater.

That night, as we ate royally once again and Larry sniffed around to find out what kind of article I'd be writing about a salmon lodge that had no fishing water of its own and some other defects I was considering how to ease into the conversation, a very muscular individual arrived and engaged our host in animated negotiations, at the unsatisfactory conclusion of which the very muscular individual lifted our host by the neck and held him suspended, perhaps to better emphasize his key negotiating point: "I'll fockin' kill yez."

As we took these to be private business matters we thought it best to absent ourselves—Bob hid in the bedroom, Ted behind the couch, I fled to the porch—but given the volume, persistence, and proximity of the extended negotiations we came to understand that this lodge wasn't exactly Larry's, that for a year or so he had been leasing it from the very muscular individual without properly consummating the lease, so to speak, with cash.

Larry, keen on not being fockin' killed, tried to borrow money from us, but the guides, who as it turned out Larry had not paid either, had already cleaned us out. And, well, given the episode of the unpaid guides, some of us were ambivalent about the fockin' killing of Larry.

Finally, Larry drove to the town's ATM and returned with sufficient cash to keep from being fockin' killed, and after an uncomfortable evening and a silent breakfast, we drove back to Maine, stopping at the West Branch en route to decompress and wash away the taste of fraud with an evening rise.

As we broke down our rods in the gathering dark, Bob apologized once again for dragging us off on what he described as a horrific experience, and we assured him once again that any experience that doesn't fockin' kill you leaves you stronger—and laughing.

Then Bob asked the same question Larry had asked as we'd left that morning: "Do you think you'll write about this trip?"

"Someday," I said. "Someday."

All of these stories are about good trips, even those that on the surface seem otherwise. For all levered me away from my closeted little world of small streams, tiny fly rods, and miniature brook trout and forced me off into the greater world beyond, meeting new people, seeing new country, trying new things, learning something. That's what travel, and fly fishing, is all about.

14

Appleknocker Time

The sea speaks a language polite people never repeat. It is a colossal scavenger slang and has no respect.

—CARL SANDBURG, "Two Nocturnes"

*I*n this marina snack bar in a salty little corner of Rhode Island, the past lives on—creaking chrome-and-Naugahyde swivel stools, press-letter wall menus advertising fried this and grilled that at Johnson-administration prices, a wisecracking cook/waitress/ social commentator presiding over a faded green counter and a gleaming ancient grill with a five-degree starboard list: every-boomer's yesteryear preserved within a multilayered amber of Fryolater fumes, tobacco smoke, and other forms of hot air.

We're after a particular kind of hot air this morning, me and Ed, the kind that vents only from local fishermen who've known each other since childhood and are shamefully abusing caffeine. We've come to eavesdrop, to gather intelligence, a task made easier because

147

Ed has been swiveling around on one of these stools all his life,
thus cloaking me—an obvious outlander wearing the many-
pocketed attire of Fly-Fishing Dude and talking like Jed Clampett
meets Percy Kilbride—under his indigenous umbrella of confi-
dentiality and providing whispered translations for the rapid-fire
local dialect.

I'm levering a gratuitous slab of butter into a poppy-seed
muffin the size and shape of a baby's butt, nodding sagely as the
cook/waitress/social commentator says I better not have to pee in
a bottle 'cause with all those poppy seeds I'll register 100-proof
junkie, and trying to decode what Old Guy—stubble, Camels, two
flannel shirts, hip boots rolled down at the knees, bacon and eggs—
is saying to Young Guy—stubble, Marlboros, two flannel shirts, hip
boots rolled down at the knees, chorizos and eggs:

Old Guy: "How'dja do ovah-da weegh-end?"

Young Guy: "Naw bad. Went ovah da Noopaht 'n hooghed up
wid a real Hoodsie from th' college."

A Hoodsie, I remember from a long-ago experimental resi-
dence in Boston, under whose cultural and dairy-products hege-
mony Little Rhodie partially falls, is both a sweet little ice cream
cup and a deceptively young female who is petite, pert, and just
possibly promiscuous.

Old Guy: "Heh heh heh, ya dutty bastid. So'dya do ennithin' up
th' shaw yestaday?"

"Couple appleknockahs . . ."

Appleknockers? A new one for me. All kinds of firmly prurient
images are bobbing through my mind when Young Guy finishes
his sentence:

". . . and a nice bunneeda."

Bonito? Fish! After five coffees and a muffin's worth of who did
what to whom and who wants to do what to whom and who did
what once again to the Red Sox, they're finally talking about an

activity that in my declining years arouses more than academic interest.

I lean toward Ed: "Appleknockers?"

And Ed says, "False albacore. Little tunny. They come inshore with the fall, mid-October, when the apples start falling off the trees: appleknockers."

I'm still trying to get Appleknockers Version One out of my head when Ed bangs back the rest of his coffee and says, "So let's go look for some."

As is usual when I go fishing in this tumultuous era of Global Warming, it's blowing southeast fifteen to twenty-five and the barometer's unwinding like a cheap clock. Ed's friend Mike Laptew, a Rhode Island filmmaker whose video *Stripers in Paradise* is as good an education in Northeast saltwater fishing as can be found, is lugging his cameras and diving equipment aboard the *Fly Swatter*, Ed's Shamrock 27, eyeing the squall line swallowing the horizon and talking himself out of going underwater today. Ed's waving around a coffee cup with one hand and a dripping gas nozzle with the other and saying what every fisherman who's just driven three hundred miles loves to hear: "Geeze. Ya shudda come down last week. The stripahs were just tearin' up everything."

I'd met Ed Hughes the year before, when he was guiding on Midway Island. We'd become friends—not because he'd talked me through landing a seventy-pound giant trevally but because we had important stuff in common: We'd both been commercial fishermen, we could recite verbatim most crucial Monty Python episodes, and we'd attended the same Jeff Beck concert at the old Boston Teaparty way back in the good old days.

Ed started saltwater fly fishing in the good old days, too, back when it was considered beyond eccentric, at least in New England. By 1985 he was showing so many people how to fly fish for stripers and bluefish and even bluefin tuna—this back when a nine-weight was a serious fly rod and the favored saltwater reel was a Pflueger 1498 soaked in WD-40—he figured he might as well charge for it, and he's been guiding ever since. Not today, though. Today and tomorrow are just for fun.

Fun isn't the first word that occurs to me as we clear Point Judith, cross wakes with the Block Island ferry, and green water slams into the windscreen. Futile comes to mind, not to mention idiotic, but a burst of optimism fueled by caffeine—everything is fueled by caffeine in rapid Rhode Island, where kids are raised on milk boosted with Autocrat Coffee Syrup instead of a squirt of Hershey's chocolate like the rest of the country—forces out a grudging Why not to Ed's "Ready for this?" and he squirrels up to the fly bridge and starts looking for signs of fish.

In this fertile little crescent of ocean framed by Martha's Vineyard, Buzzards Bay, Narragansett Bay, and Block Island Sound, fishing the fall migration is very much a search-and-destroy operation. Sharp eyes posted high radar around the horizon for signs of swirling birds that mark schools of baitfish ravaged by stripers and blues and bonito and little tunny binge-fattening for the long journey south to the warmer waters off Virginia and North Carolina.

In these square-sided four-foot seas it's hard to see anything, never mind signs of feeding fish, but soon Ed's stomping on the overhead and pointing and hollering into the wind like a caffeinated Ahab cursing Moby Dick, and as we head for a point just off the seawall I lurch to the stern with my fly rod. A dozen laughably ineffectual casts later and I've had enough—try to imagine fly casting into a wind tunnel while being involuntarily pistoned by an arrhythmic trampoline and firehosed by rain and spray—so Mike steps up with a light spinning rig dangling a blue-and-white Acme Needl-eel. Half a dozen casts and he's into the first of two lightning-fast bonito in the eight-pound range, one released, one knocked on the head for supper. Unlike little tunny, which rival blue sharks for sheer culinary loathsomeness despite A. J. McClane's claim in *Fish Cookery* that they're good if brined and smoked (I mean, what isn't?), bonito are prime eats, needing little more than a squirt of lemon, a grind of pepper, and a swipe with extra-virgin before hitting the Weber.

Now it's my turn, and on my third retrieve the rod jerks water-ward and ten-pound mono melts off the little Van Staal like a Hoodsie on a hot plate. I'm convinced I've hung one of those fast-attack submarines from New London that we're not supposed to know go forty-five knots underwater, but fifteen minutes and four equally blistering runs later and we're releasing a nine-pound false albacore—for its size, the strongest fish I've ever seen, and the fastest fish of *any* size I've ever seen: way faster than a bonefish. It looks like a scale-model tuna, which of course it is, albeit tenu-ously related familially and completely unrelated culinarily to the white-meat albacore that Charlie Tuna hawks on TV. And like those fast-attack subs, appleknockers really do go forty-five knots.

I don't think there's a better fly-rod quarry on the planet, at least if you define *better* as the ability to send an angler's heartbeat racing out of control, even an angler not revved up on caffeine. And unlike tarpon or giant trevally or the larger tuna, little tunny and bonito fight just long enough to be fun without devolving into a wearying exercise in heavy lifting that leaves you singing "Song of the Volga Boatmen" and gobbling outdated painkillers left over from your root canal.

We make a few more drifts along the seawall, casting blind now, but the fish have disappeared. With the weather worsening and the muffins wearing off, we decide to do what Real Fishermen do when uncooperative fish and climatological adversity sap angling of its fun: Go eat pizza and drink beer. Then we need to get some rest, Ed says, "for tonight we pahty."

*   *   *

It's less like a party than a late-night convocation of an obscure religious sect or an off-Broadway adaptation of *Night of the Living Dead* performed by a secretive nocturnal angling society, with the initiates arriving by ones and twos through anonymous backyards belonging to the shuttered summer homes of stockbrokers gone home to the city. Like moths, we're drawn toward the pale green glow of security lights shining on what looks like a Montana spring creek, only lined with squared granite blocks and dotted with spruce little Olde Newe Englande faux fisherman's wharves built more for Ikea lawn furniture than bait barrels.

This is the outlet to Potter's Pond, one of the many saltwater ponds that split the coast hereabouts and which serve as fecund food factories for the baitfish that make this area one of the hottest saltwater fishing destinations on the East Coast.

As the tide starts to ebb, more anglers drift in.

"Zatchoo Ed?"

"Yeah. Yadoinennything?"

"Nah. Seen some. Nothin' takin'."

The front has passed through and the night is dead still; the water is perfectly transparent, and tiny silver flashes show deep against the eelgrass-furred bottom. Then comes a huge *splooonk* just upstream from the highway bridge, and a dozen ghostly green anglers stop waving their rods and turn to stare. To me it sounded like one of the perforated and large-panted teenagers swilling coffee on the bridge tossed in a mailbox to register untargeted societal displeasure, but then the chain-letter whisper of "stripah—big-ass stripah" finally reaches me. Maybe it's a party after all.

Maybe, but not for us. The big splooonks are coming more often now as stripers chase to the surface anchovies and immature menhaden frantic to be anywhere but where they are, but we can't get them to look at our flies and keep shuffling through boxes looking for The Key.

On the opposite bank, two guys tossing small Rapalas catch a couple of stripers—schoolies in the eight- to ten-pound range— and this sends us scrambling for poppers and sliders, figuring if we can't match the menhaden at least we can match the Rapalas.

Then a Rhode Island coastal warden materializes from nowhere and I figure we're busted—I mean this *looks* as close to criminal trespass as anything I'll ever admit to—but he's just checking things out: "Hey Ed, zatchoo? Yadoinennything?"

"Nothin'. Guys got a couple on Rapalas. They won't lookit our flies."

The warden's theory—that in the dead-still night the security lights cause our fly lines to cast big threatening shadows over the ice-clear water while the thin monofilament is more or less invisible—seems logical to me, and I think of those new transparent striper lines sitting at home on my desk, waiting for a trial.

Meanwhile the tide's draining fast and we haven't heard a splooonk in fifteen minutes. One by one the rods stop waving, and the only movements that break the creek's cathedral calm are the pale green bobbings of Styrofoam coffee cups fluorescing under metal-halide lights.

The next day dawns clear with a hard northwesterly that promises to peter out by noon, when Ed has to meet paying customers. For me this will be a short day. As we leave the harbor, birds are working isolated schools of baitfish just outside the boat channel, and we take a few small schoolies and a couple of shad on a skinny blue-and-white anchovy pattern.

We have a peek outside the seawall and find the seas from yesterday's southeasterlies battling it out with today's northwesterlies, so we duck back inside and cruise around, slurping coffee from the thermos and looking for action. We aren't long finding it, as birds converge from all directions on a mammoth school of anchovies being ripped up by something. We drift alongside the boiling water and I throw cast after cast before finally connecting with what turns out to be a mackerel not much longer than my fly. Then it's no longer anchovies being chased into the air by tinker mackerel but tinker mackerel being chased into the air by something much bigger. I cast again and the sea explodes, and as the line heads for the horizon Ed hollers down from the fly bridge, "Jeezusgawdalmightychrist what a stripah. His tail's gotta be bettah'n a foot across." I'm braced hard against the rail and the striper's shaking his head at the end of a long, long line, then he turns to run toward the boat, but even with a major coffee buzz I can't reel fast enough and the line goes slack.

Outside the seawall more baitfish are being ripped to pieces—"bunneeda," Ed declares from on high—and we head out and chase the school along the wall. Finally a nine-pounder grabs my fly and lights off his afterburners, making five rapid runs that start at a hundred yards and decrease by twenty yards per dash until he's boatside. As soon as he's off I'm into a much-bigger one, and I'm almost instantly looking at three wraps shy of a bare spool where two hundred yards of backing used to be. I get him down to fifty yards, then he starts wrapping up in the leader like a shark and quickly saws through the twelve-pound tippet. "Musta been a big albie," Ed decides between gulps of coffee, then our watches say paying customers coming, and it's time for me to head back to Maine.

A week later Ed calls and says "Geeze, ya should come back down. The stripahs are just tearin' up everything." And I say Sure, I'll be right down. As soon as I get out of caffeine detox.

15

Cabo Wabo

The real picture of how it had been there and how we had been there was in our minds, bright with sun and wet with sea water and blue or burned, and the whole crusted over with exploring thought. . . . The brown Indians and the gardens of the sea, and the beer and the work, they were all one thing and we were that one thing too.

—JOHN STEINBECK,
The Log from the Sea of Cortez

Fifteen million years ago the San Andreas Fault, diverting briefly from its dream of uniting Los Angeles and San Francisco, split off Baja California from mainland Mexico. From space Baja resembles the languorously splayed leg of some great earth mother, from whose womb pours the Colorado River and its cargo of eroded continental spine, nourishment for the fertile Sea of Cortez.

155

"The exposed rocks had looked rich with life under the lowering tide," wrote John Steinbeck in his weirdly riveting *The Log from the Sea of Cortez*, "but they were more than that: they were ferocious with life. There was an exuberant fierceness in the littoral here, a vital competition for existence."

In 1941, when Steinbeck and Ed Ricketts—"Doc" of *Cannery Row*—cruised through here on a rambling voyage of biological discovery, continental coda Cabo San Lucas was a "sad little town" slumped around a malodorous tuna cannery. Now it boasts Mexico's most vibrant economy—a humming jet-set tourist playground that smells of sunblock, fresh concrete, and money.

At land's end the pea-green Sea of Cortez meets the vast blue Pacific, and like ecosystem boundaries everywhere this happy confluence forms a hunter's paradise. Here swarm large marine predators of every kind, including an artificially amphibious bipedal mammal. More than a thousand sport-fishing boats fill the harbor at Cabo San Lucas, everything from modest outboard-powered *pangas* carrying casual vacationing line-wetters to sleekly lethal Ryboviches packed with purposeful bronze trophy hunters manhandling reels the size of halyard winches and rods as thick as your thumb.

Until recently, Macho Cabo has had little patience with effete light-tackle anglers and wussy fly fishers. But in the past few years a couple of local outfitters have begun tailoring both equipment and temperament to these quixotic romanticists, who turn probability into slim chance to satisfy personal definitions of fair chase— and manage to drop some fairly serious bucks along the way.

I'm here fishing with Baja Anglers, which operates a pair of Glacier Bay catamarans from their fly-fisherly new headquarters overlooking the marina. Lightning fast and remarkably stable, with a padded waist-level pulpit forward where you can brace yourself and cast freely in rough seas, these tubby fiberglass cats are real fly-fishing machines, with the speed and sea-keeping ability to fish twenty or thirty miles offshore in more safety and comfort than was ever possible in the lean sharklike *pangas* that put to sea as encrusted with macho-man attitude and fly-line tangling impedimenta as a Tijuana Taxi.

As an habitual fly fisherman, I've long dreamed of catching a marlin—"a beast," wrote Hunter Thompson in *The Curse of Lono*, that can "rip your arm-bones right out of their sockets, then leap right into the boat and snap your spine like a toothpick." And while blue or black marlin nearing half a ton are a bit much for a mostly trout fisherman to be dueling *mano a mano* with a fly rod, striped marlin, which average only around 125 pounds, are the perfect quarry—a billfish with training wheels. And Cabo San Lucas in January and February is the perfect place to catch them.

Usually.

I confess to being the unequivocal reincarnation of Joe Btfsplk, the gloomy geek in *Li'l Abner* followed everywhere by his own evil weather. True to form, I arrived at this tropical Pacific outpost towing a perfect North Atlantic gale—a globe-girdling monster that lashed California with rain measured in feet and froze the winter vegetable crop all across Mexico and Florida.

In this dry desert town of year-round eighty-degree days and sixty-five-degree nights, the cold windswept rains sent Cabo residents into shock. Shivering Mexicans clustered in doorways and turned sad chocolate eyes toward the boiling gray-green sky, crossing themselves and shaking their heads in disbelief and singing long mournful songs. California tourists—obvious by their sleekly trendy clothing and sparkling toothy smiles—seemed equally stricken by the weather and were looking for someone to blame.

But for the many Canadians who inexplicably call Baja Sur their winter home, this was merely another splendid day in paradise, and they splashed merrily along in oilskins and boots, swinging their arms and whistling, dreaming of ice and snow and poutine.

I huddled at Cheeseburger Cheeseburger, a waterfront American-theme bistro, plotting strategy with Baja Anglers' manager Grant Hartman, a Texas expatriate and a sixteen-year veteran of Mexico's fly-fishing subculture, and Craig Boulden, my fishing compadre for this trip and a longtime guide in Alaska and Wyoming. Screw the weather, we finally decided: Marlin are easiest to catch on the surface when the weather's awful, when the roiled sea makes these sight-feeders feel secure and daring.

Usually.

But after six fruitless hours off soundings, with the gusts passing thirty-five knots, the seas cresting six feet, and the forty-footers all heading for the barn, we finally gave up too and slogged back to Cabo, pounding like a pile driver and shipping green water all the way. From the VHF we learned that only our guide Joel's father, on the thirty-five-foot *Minerva II*, had taken fish, two small marlin on deep-drifted live bait.

The next day dawned cloudy and windy, with the cold swirl of green water that wedged aside the warm blue Humboldt current doubtless driving the marlin even deeper. We tried trolling the surf for roosterfish, even though we knew it was too cold and the seas too rough to get close enough to shore to put our flies where they needed to be.

We found no roosters, but we were quickly into sierra mackerel—savage little snap-toothed wolves that shredded flies and chewed through wire leaders like piranhas. "This golden fish with brilliant blue spots is shaped like a trout," wrote Steinbeck, and "its meat is white and delicate and sweet." With an eye toward supper, we killed and filleted a few in the five-pound range and crowded them into the ice chest alongside the stash of Coronas.

Seeking bigger game, we ran twenty miles west to Golden Gate Bank, where Joel thought we might find dorado and maybe a marlin. Nearing a buoy, we slowed and trailed back lures and flies. One minute Craig's rubber squid bubbled and wheezed across the surface, the next minute it was clamped in the jaws of a miniature Moby Dick dyed psychedelic chartreuse, its leading edges flashing a brilliant electric blue as it cartwheeled six feet into the air then blistered off toward Tahiti. Craig, twenty-six years an Alaska guide and thus presumably jaded about big leaping fish, shouted an endless stream of *awesomes* and *wows*—"This is the *coolest fish!*" he kept saying over and over. Of course I was far too sophisticated to fall into such childish displays of enthusiasm. Until a twenty-pound dorado hit *my* rubber squid.

Imagine a crank-crazed Atlantic salmon with a hugely humped head and a Grateful Dead light show splashed across its side—a "startlingly beautiful fish of pure gold, pulsing and fading and changing colors," understated Steinbeck.

Now imagine me as Beavis after slamming down two pots of cappuccino and three bags of stolen Halloween candy: *Whoa!* This fish *rules!*

On the way back to Cabo the skies brightened, and the seas slowly subsided and bloomed with life: Gray whales breached ponderously and blew; playful young humpbacks leaped into the air; a distant sperm whale spouted its telltale locomotive exhaust; giant manta rays rose vertically from the sea and crashed back like garage doors thrown from helicopters; pods of spinner dolphins swept by, rippling the sea like serpents. Frigate birds hung suspended from an endless blue sky, still fishing as we headed home to our rented condo for cold beer and sierra. "Simply fried in big hunks," wrote

Steinbeck, "it is the most delicious fish of all." Sierra is that, and equally delicious on a fly rod.

The next day brought light westerlies and clear skies. Spread across ten miles of undulating painted ocean, a loose-knit squadron of tiny white boats trolled in random patterns while whales and dolphins and manta rays flashed in and out of the glaring sun.

We became lost in the scene, hypnotized by droning engines and inactivity. Suddenly a fat snout tossing up a PT-boat bow wave charged the teaser—a giant dorado, incandescing blue and gold and big enough to swallow the twenty-pounders we took yesterday. Joel cut the engine and frantically stripped in the teaser, screaming *Cast cast cast* and standing in the only spot on the boat that made it impossible for us to cast. Craig launched his fourteen-weight into the air and snared the VHF antenna, and I grabbed for my cameras and tossed them at the ice chest, and suddenly the fish was gone—laughing hysterically, no doubt. Just like us.

Then bursts of excited Spanish crackled over the VHF. Joel leaped to the console, yelling *Hang on* and jamming the throttles wide open, and we hurtled from wave to wave at forty-five knots toward a spot on the ocean fifteen miles away, where something monumental clearly was happening.

Four boats drifted around a weed-covered milk crate, and a dozen crazed anglers were hot into dorado. The water literally boiled with them—swirling and flashing as far as the eye could see. I grabbed the lumbering fourteen-weight and, with all the grace of tossing a wet turkey off the end of a cue stick, flopped a huge billfish fly in the ocean's general direction. A big bull dorado nailed the fly in midair, tail-walking and somersaulting then vanishing, to reappear far in the distance twisting high in the sun.

We took dorado after dorado, me in the bow, Craig in the stern, with Joel running excitedly back and forth getting in the way and jabbering maniacally. Then something hit that felt massive the way a shark feels massive, boring straight for the mile-deep bottom with the fourteen-weight bent double and me trying not to get hauled overboard headfirst. Finally I pumped to the surface what looked like a twenty-pound bluegill wearing Desert Storm camouflage: a tripletail, flaring his fins and burning with rage. I lost him boatside and was actually relieved, at least until Grant told me they taste even better than sierra or dorado.

Hungry for more dorado, I wound up the fourteen-weight and sent a mighty twenty-foot backcast straight into a big sportfisherman that had sidled up unseen behind us, its decks crowded with burnished buxom women in cocktail dresses and florid men in unflattering shorts, all madly winching aboard dorado with giant tuna rods. We had become a city on the sea at least thirty boats strong, with more converging from all directions. Boats drifted into one another, lines tangled and retangled, mono wound up into props, and everywhere slashing gaffs transformed acrobatic dorado into slabs of dead meat.

"*Ohmigod whatta fish,*" someone screeched nearby, as Joel gently unhooked a monster dorado and slid it back into the sea. "*Christ, he threw it BACK; are youse guys CRAZY?*" another yelled. It seemed pointless to explain that yesterday we'd killed two dorado for tonight's supper with Grant and his gracious wife, Gisel; that we had no reason to kill anymore. This crowd was not into moderation. It wanted *blood.* Craig and I exchanged glances: Time to go.

We headed north and trolled throughout the day, and although we saw two marlin we could not interest them in our yanqui flies. Craig caught another dorado while casting big orange flies into a trash line filled with bloated puffers drifting by like loofahs, shrimp-trawler discards, Joel said, and we both caught more hot-rod sierra on orange-and-white bucktails in the surf beneath the old lighthouse and wished, as we ground them in on our twelve-weights, that we had brought whippy little six-weights to do them justice.

Too soon our time in Cabo was done, and as a lone humpback whale spiraled majestically skyward a quarter mile off the trademark Cabo arch, I thought of Steinbeck's words: "The very air here is miraculous, and outlines of reality change with the moment. The sky sucks up the land and disgorges it. A dream hangs over the whole region, a brooding kind of hallucination."

Los Cabos does seem to dwell at the edge of unreal, a polarized Kodachrome vision that everything here is almost too good to be true. Compared with a better-known tourist magnet halfway down another dangling continental protuberance far to the east, Los Cabos seems more peaceful, more affordable, marginally more tasteful, and endlessly more entertaining. And although its nightlife, like Florida's, runs knee-deep in alcohol and the hormonal secretions of American adolescents crowding drunkenly into shrieking local clubs like Sammy Hagar's Cabo Wabo, Cabo is at least free from giant three-fingered rats shrieking "It's a Small World After All."

Its tourist-based economy awash with money guarantees a constabulary sternly determined to preserve the Pax Mammonicus and not, like police forces in other parts of Mexico increasingly seem inclined to do, slit your throat and part-out your rent-a-car. Sugar-sand beaches filled with delicate Sally Lightfoot crabs skittering about and sleek oiled women trolling for melanomas stretch as far as the eye cares to see, and when fishing grows stale you can spend hours lounging there or around the harbor sipping Coronas and eating sierra or tripletail or whatever you wish to bring in from the sea and trade, for four dollars plus drinks, to any one of a dozen thatch-roofed waterfront joints that will barbecue your fish with lemon and garlic and deliver them to your table along with onion rings, salsa, guacamole, and steamily fragrant tortillas. You can lean back and soak up the sun—it shines most of the time even when I'm in town—while well-buffed tourists stroll past mega-yachts buddying up to the quay and dainty white egrets spider down mooring lines to spear anchovies driven aloft by the mammoth snook lurking beneath the piers.

And then there are those dorado—dolphinfish, mahimahi, call them what you will—truly the coolest fish that swims.

I hear that marlin swim in the waters off Cabo San Lucas, but somehow I don't really care.

16

Defenders of Midway

And a good south wind sprung up behind;
The Albatross did follow,
And every day, for food or play,
Came to the mariners' hollo!

—SAMUEL TAYLOR COLERIDGE,
"The Rime of the Ancient Mariner"

It's almost too surreal, this scene. I'm leaning against an ironwood tree and painfully scribbling in a Flintstones notebook, watching the sun sink deep into yesterday and trying to defend my Mont Blanc from a gang of puffball albatross chicks that mean to have it. Between here and the sunset lies the International Dateline, 140 miles west across the flinty blue Pacific. A mile away, booming white surf traces the coral-crusted rim of an extinct volcano, within which nestles an apple-green lagoon rippled here and there by endangered Hawaiian monk seals, spinner dolphins, green turtles, and the ghosts of a naval battle that was the end of

165

the beginning for one great power and the beginning of the end for another. Curving peripherally into the dusk is an opalescent crescent of powdery beach dotted with thousands of socializing albatross—bobbing and weaving and elegantly sniffing their armpits, chattering like air wrenches loosening lug nuts and blatting with heads thrown back like tone-deaf jazzmen wailing on kazoos. Overhead, beneath the sweeping coma of the Hale-Bopp Comet, thousands of black noddies and white fairy terns swirl through the soft divide between night and day, aerobatic yins and yangs in a Hitchcock sky.

Lurking just beyond the reef is a fish so aggressive even sharks shy off when they blast into view—a fish the Hawaiians call *ulua,* the giant trevally, GT. Imagine a steroid-crazed cross between a permit and a piranha that can reach 190 pounds. Imagine whole schools of them, snapping at boat propellers and team-ramming any sharks that dare come sniffing up a chum slick they've claimed as their own. Imagine a fish that, in an hour and a half at the business end of a fourteen-weight, can turn perfectly useful hands with evolutionarily superior opposable thumbs into primitive claws that can barely grip a pen, never mind defend it from a jostling crowd of rooster-size delinquents.

Here on Midway Atoll—where I am about to lose an overpriced ink pen to the snatting bills of goofy-looking squeeze-toy albatrosslings that methodically decorate their nests with shiny plastic novelties while Mom and Dad scour the ocean a thousand miles around for squid, small fish, and ancient mariners—the *ulua* is the boss dog, the apex predator, the meanest mutha around. And it's likely to remain so. In crowded, hungry Hawaii, young *ulua* get snarfled up immediately upon reaching luau size, but here in unpopulated ciguatera-toxin land, eating a top-of-the-food-chain *ulua* guarantees a medevac flight twelve hundred miles southeast to the hospital in Honolulu.

This inherent toxicity kept Midway's inshore fishery a de facto catch-and-release operation even during the atoll's fifty-year sequester as a naval base. Now, with the navy gone and the arrival of civilian management, a catch-and-release advisory has hardened into official policy. Except for world-record fish killed to fulfill the IGFA's antiquated rules and a limited number of high-seas pelagics done in for chum and seaside barbecues, Midway Sport Fishing, the atoll's sole operator, defends the virtue of this near-virgin fishery against all comers. Sheer economics, cynics will sniff; the better the fishing, in these days of high-roller fly fishers searching the globe for exotic new challenges, the more outfitters can charge for it. But there's far more protecting this weird little atoll than simple economics. Everywhere you look busy parents are raising young; the very air is a hormonal miasma of nurture, permeating everything and everyone on this incubator island. Within days of arrival, even the most hard-charging results-oriented FisherMen sit sipping Coronas in the shade and radiating maternal waves, while red-tailed tropic birds and elegantly curious fairy terns circle their heads like celestial satellites orbiting St. Francis of Assisi.

Born twenty-nine million years ago, about where Kilauea now looms over the Big Island of Hawaii, the volcano that became Midway Atoll spent the intervening eons tectonically migrating north-northwest into the fertile latitude of West Palm Beach, along the way acclimating a Noah's Ark of kidnapped tropical species and creating a wet dream for fish hunters, whether they soar aloft on nine-foot wings or ride the waves aboard fiberglass sportfishermen. Inhabited only by birds and marine mammals before its discovery in 1859, later home to the Pacific Cable telegraph company, an elegant forty-five-room Pan American Flying Clipper hotel, and a grimly purposeful naval air station, Midway Atoll has lately become a wildlife sanctuary administered by the

U.S. Fish and Wildlife Service—a multiple-use demonstration project intended to prove that wildlife and people can coexist. They pretty much have to, for with once flush government coffers frittered away on gold-plated plumbing fixtures and export subsidies to multinational fast-food franchisers, Midway Atoll National Wildlife Refuge must pay its own way, in part by hosting small groups of anglers, birders, snorkelers, marine mammal researchers, and nostalgic ex-navy types drawn here, like the albatross, by Midway's mysterious magnetism.

Midway is like no other place on earth, and it is the million or so albatross—Midway's famed Gooney Birds—that make it so. When we arrived on Sand Island after a late-night flight from Lihue—planes fly in and out of Midway only after the birds are safely on their nests—we felt we'd entered not an old naval air station but an aviary. Birds were everywhere: soaring above the apron, strolling down taxiways, peering from beneath fuel trucks.

On the van ride to our rooms, our driver—a piratical-looking Philippino you'd expect to see swarming over a pearl schooner's lee rail with a cutlass in his teeth—kept stopping to nursemaid newly mobile albatross chicks who'd waddled into the road. When he'd climb back into the van after ushering one to its nest he'd beam like Buddha, and when he stopped to move aside the corpse of a chick some less cautious driver had run down, tears flowed down his cheeks in great crocodile gouts.

Outside my room in the old bachelor officers' quarters, nesting pairs lined the walkway and nestled against the wall, keening and rasping and tap-tap-tapping like little shoemakers toiling the night away. An hour or so before dawn the noise level ratcheted up, and as I went outside to investigate parental pairs began leaving their nests and ambling toward a preflight staging area on the beach, stopping every few feet to greet another converging group and bobbing their heads like conventioneering Shriners vehemently agreeing with one another. As the skies sifted the spectrum from purple to pink they began to fill from horizon to horizon with albatross, Mom and Dad circling and sweeping and heading out to sea for a long day's shopping.

All across the island thousands of walkers—young albatross returning to Midway from their seven adolescent years at sea to look for a sympathetic face with which to share their next thirty-something years—strolled hopefully about, trying out their intricate mating dances on whomever they met, including, repeatedly, me.

At an orientation meeting, Fish and Wildlife operatives filled us in on the atoll's history, natural and otherwise; they warned us about tropical infections, about always staying on paths lest we collapse the burrows of the thousands of Bonin petrels that prairie-dog the islands, about staying downwind and at least four hundred feet from the monk seals, the second most endangered marine mammal on earth. We were particularly warned, as we wobbled about the island on screeching rusty navy-issue bicycles, how easy it is to eat feathers here. Albatross weigh nine pounds and glide in for a landing at forty miles per hour, and they have not evolved the ability to compute evasion courses with converging bicyclists. Four people got coldcocked off bikes just last month, we're told.

Birds, monk seals, spinner dolphins, green turtles, timeless history. It's all enough to bring anyone to this remotest of remote spots, where you are farther from anywhere than you can be and still be somewhere, for a week of being spellbound. But in the end what brought me here, of course, was the fishing, the rumors of these giant trevally, a fish so powerful and ferocious a four-weight trout wuss like me lacks even the contextual vocabulary to describe them. So I'll rely on my friend Pete Parker, a longtime bluewater fly fisherman and the new holder of the IGFA giant trevally record for twelve-pound test. A few minutes after boating his record-book 53.8-pounder, Pete described his GT, between puffs on a celebratory Arturo Fuente, as "the finest fish of my life—better than marlin, better than sail, better than tarpon. It was the toughest fish I've ever experienced. Tougher even than a yellowfin tuna."

Tough? I've been a farmer, a truck driver, and a commercial fisherman, but my toughest job ever was the hour and a half I spent fighting my own big *ulua*—at 70.3 pounds a new world fly-tackle record for sixteen-pound tippet.

Well, almost.

We'd had both boats rafted up and a good chum slick going, with hundreds of fish—bluefin trevally, *butaguchi,* jacks, rudder-fish—swirling and flashing near the surface. Then suddenly our flock skittered off in all directions; Gaffney yelled "GTs! GTs!" grabbed a big surf rod, and began flailing away with an enormous hookless popper, and the sea absolutely erupted with huge speedboat wakes slashing back and forth, spray and blood and chopped-up fish flying everywhere. I tossed in a big Pete's Slider and dragged it jaggedly through the maelstrom, crossing wakes with Gaffney's twisting teaser. Ten yards astern the sea humped up and a hog-size shape leaped head-high—jaws agape, fins flaring, inflamed red eyes jutting out and rolling around maniacally—and came down atop the slider. Then, with a jerk and a heave and a splash like a Volkswagen-size beaver pulling the alarm, it quite literally headed for the horizon. In not much more time than it is taking to scribble these words in my Barney Rubble notebook and deflect another clacking bill from this fancy pen a well-heeled relative thought might make a nice gift for a writer, I had close to three hundred yards of backing running parallel to the ocean and a tenuous connection, far off in the distance, with an elemental force of nature.

This was not going to be a pretty fight, as Pete's had been earlier in the day. Ed Hughes—the other inshore guide here, along with Rick Gaffney from Kona—said, "It was the best I've ever seen that fish fought. Pete was as calm and poised as a saint the whole time, even when an osprey bonked into his taut fly line and did a 360. Pete was in the zone, man."

But I wasn't in a zone. I was in trouble. Ed said, "You want that fish, man, we gotta go after it. I don't wanna getcha nervous, but that's a record fish for certain."

So we slipped the anchor buoy and angled up the fly line, Ed taking it slow and coaching me like a midwife at a breech birth, me pumping and reeling like crazy, the fish imperturbably bulling its way ever farther out to sea. Six times I fought that GT to the rail, and six times it rallied and sped off with a boat-soaking splash.

Finally I had it alongside and finning weakly on its back, and as a half-dozen reef sharks circled in cautiously for their one sure chance at revenge against this bad-tempered bully of the atoll, Ed said, "That's a world record, man. I can bring it aboard or let it go, but if I let it go weak like that the sharks'll kill it for sure. It's up to you."

I'm not a fan of world records. They're fine for achievement-oriented folks, but something about them just doesn't sit right with meek and mild-mannered me: the chase, the hunger, the anxious sifting through record books for breakable subcategories of unpopular species. But then . . .

But then I hadn't sought a world record; a world record had sought me. And I'd almost certainly never luck into another one.

"Kill it."

Ed shooed away the sharks, heaved it aboard, and knocked it in the head with a baseball bat, and we headed back for port, where we hung the GT from the gallows, confirmed the weight, took smiling, handshaking photographs, did the whole Manly Male world-record dance. And when we went looking for the tippet and fly to send to IGFA, we found it clenched firmly in the mouth of a five-pound rudderfish stuck deep in my big *ulua*'s throat, apparently swallowed whole at the same instant the rudderfish took my slider. My *ulua* wasn't even hooked; it was just damned if it would let go of that rudderfish. Without Ed's prescient boat-handling and coaching, and my own strong back, weak mind, and blind luck, I'd have never gotten it near the boat. And from IGFA's viewpoint? I caught my big *ulua* on live bait.

So I'm not a world-record holder after all; just a middle-aged man with fish-wrecked hands sitting in the middle of the world's largest albatross colony and fighting fuzzy hand puppets and their randy young-adult reinforcements for possession of a pretentious pen. And remembering the fish of my life. I guess that's enough.

Well, almost.

I wish I could look back on the day and say I'd been as classy as Eddy Sisom, a salmon-charter skipper from Sitka, Alaska, who a few hours earlier on sixteen-pound conventional tackle took a hundred-plus-pounder that was easily a world line-class record. Eddy let it go, God bless him. I'd like to think I killed my *ulua* because it was belly-up exhausted and the dozen or so reef sharks menacing the boat would have torn it to pieces. But that's just a cheap defense of a tenuous position. The truth is, once it became apparent this was a record-class fish, I never wanted anything so badly in my life.

By the way, if you're keeping score, that was three record-breaking *ulua* from one boat in one day of fishing at Midway. In the off season.

Of course more than just *ulua* cruise the waters around Midway. In fact, it would almost be easier to list the species that don't swim these waters than the ones that do. Out beyond the hundred-fathom curve, the endless Pacific teems with bad-ass billfish of all kinds, along with wahoo, mahimahi, and shoals of yellowfin, big-eye, and skipjack tuna.

The nearshore waters are equally alive with GTs, amberjacks, reef sharks, kawakawas, groupers, and a host of pugnacious reef species including bluefin trevally and *butaguchi*—pig-*ulua,* thick-lip trevally. These gut-busters run from six to sixteen pounds, but tie in to one on a ten-weight and you'll swear they weigh three times that. After a day of catching *butaguchi* I felt as I did my first week of navy boot camp, when I was slow learning the relationship between smart-ass comments and push-ups.

Although adventurous fly fishers here use ten-weights, Midway is really fourteen-weight land, since you never know what'll end up on the end of your line. One day Pete Turnbull, an intense San Franciscan in our party, had on an eight-pound *butaguchi* when a huge crashing wake tore out from beneath the remains of the old cargo pier and sent his thick-lip flying—an amberjack in the hundred-pound range on ambush patrol. When hooked, GTs, AJs, and *butaguchi* alike head for the bottom and its twisted labyrinth of coral and war wreckage. To land these fish you have to keep their heads up, and that places a premium on backbone, both yours and your rod's. Of course you'll lose most of them even with a four-teen-weight, and often you'll lose the fourteen-weight, too; in the week I was on Midway, three brand-new rods blew up on fish, showering the boats with shrapnel, profanity, and laughter.

If your personal vision of fly fishing centers around drifting a fragile *Baetis* imitation through a pellucid glide, this brand of nearshore saltwater fishing will lend new perspective to the phrase *dead drift,* for the hatch you're matching here comes from a chum bucket, and the only thing you'd recognize as flies have fat green bodies and gather around the chum-chopping block in enormous buzzing clouds. With the exception of Pete's Propeller Head, a big billfish fly with a hand-twisted copper propeller radiating weird come-hither vibrations in all directions, our best flies here imitated dead-drifting hunks of dead meat, like Ed's Chum Fly, a mostly red marabou concoction that closely approximated the chunks of *Thunnus albacares* that were our most effective chum and, with a little wasabi sauce, our favorite evening meal. Figuring Tokyo sashimi prices, I'm guessing we ate a thousand bucks' worth of prime yellowfin tuna every night and over the week chummed with half a million dollars' worth of leftovers, giving whole new meanings to both conspicuous consumption and elegant angling— just another facet of Midway's wacky charm.

As I lay me down under the ironwood tree, nursing my wounds and writing these words and looking out over a peaceful land where birdkind and mankind live together in a Looney Tunes egalitarianism, my mind keeps drifting back to 1942, when thousands fought and died for these two magical islets. Signs of conflict are still here if you look around: the old seaplane base's shell-pitted apron, crumbling makeshift pillboxes hidden along the beach, the bombed-out bombproof command post. Near this tree, grim sailors and marines once looked out over this same lagoon, searching for the first wave of bombers from Admiral Nagumo's hitherto unstoppable First Air Fleet. I wonder if they had time to worry a bit about the albatross and the countless other rare birds that call these islands home. Surely they, like today's tight-knit little human community, felt a beatific bond with these most inoffensive and entertaining of all God's creatures. Surely they felt them worth defending along with motherhood, apple pie, and the girls they left behind.

It's a peaceful scene today on Midway Atoll, but I suspect that somewhere within the Washington Beltway calculating eyes are looking this way, wondering if these islands might be *good* for something: an air-force missile range, perhaps, or a toxic waste dump—even a wildlife sanctuary from which the Philistine public is excluded and only select government biologists are allowed, never mind that this ivory-tower isolationism slowly erodes the only protection anything of value has in these days of diminished resources and pusillanimous politicians: a concerned and vocal constituency.

Half a century ago, the only thing standing between the largest fleet Imperial Japan ever put to sea and America's West Coast were these four square miles of sand and guano, defended by a handful of old five-inch guns, obsolete Brewster Buffalo fighters, and the carriers *Yorktown*, *Enterprise*, and *Hornet*, tipped off by navy code breakers and lying in ambush just to the north. Now Midway is defended only by a thin trickle of divers, bird-watchers, eco-tourists, and fly fishers—people who somehow find their way here, fall in love with this indescribable place, and carry it away in their hearts.

Judging from animated breakfast conversations with, among others, a retired high-society doctor and his wife, a marine colonel who fought at Guadalcanal, a famous Denver wildlife photographer, a Seattle ornithologist, and the new refuge manager who abandoned a top Washington post to come here and live life closer to the bone, these new defenders of Midway are as tenacious as ever the sailors and marines were half a century ago, as ferocious as the big *ulua* that cruise the reef, defending their turf from all comers.

I'd hate to be the bonehead bureaucrat who's dumb enough to mess with them.

17

Ursa Major

*On the twenty-first of June we had bad rainy
weather, with so thick a fog that we could not
see our way: about ten o'clock at night, however,
it became fine and clear, and the Sun shone
very bright; indeed it did not set all that
night, which was a convincing proof that we
were then considerably to the North of the
Arctic Circle.*
—SAMUEL HEARNE,
*A Journey from Prince of Wales Fort in
Hudson's Bay to the Northern Ocean*

*P*inwheeling endlessly around the immovable anchor of
Polaris, the stars of Ursa Major and Ursa Minor—the great
and lesser bears—dominate the Arctic sky, defining the High
North as surely as the aurora and for centuries exerting a magnetic
influence over humankind.

Sprawling across the Arctic Circle far below its namesake con-
stellation lies Great Bear Lake, which has magnetic properties of its

own. Around thirty-five hundred years ago, Paleo-Eskimos were drawn to live around this verdant oasis in an austere landscape. Later came the Athapaskans and then the Dene, who still hunt and fish this vast inland sea, at some thirteen thousand square miles the fourth largest lake in North America.

On his 1771 trek from Hudson Bay to the Coppermine River and the Arctic Ocean, British explorer Samuel Hearne passed through Great Bear and, to the south, Great Slave Lakes, where he and his Chipewyan guides took lake trout "of the largest size I ever saw: some that were caught by my companions could not, I think, be less than thirty-five or forty pounds weight."

In 1819-22, during his search for the Northwest Passage, Sir John Franklin traveled through Great Bear to the Coppermine, and in his expedition of 1825-27 wintered at Fort Franklin, at the southern tip of Great Bear. From this staging area, Dr. John Richardson traveled north to the Coppermine, mapping the Arctic coast around Coronation Gulf before returning to winter at Great Bear.

The accounts of Franklin and other early European visitors to this "barren land," as Franklin called it, tell of unbelievable hardships: death, madness, murder, starvation, even cannibalism.

How things change with time.

The captain's voice crackled over the intercom: "We've just crossed the Arctic Circle and are beginning our descent into Plummer's Great Bear Lodge. Please fasten your seat belts and return your seat backs and tray tables to the full upright and locked position."

In the world of North Country lodges, Plummer's is in a category all its own. Here you arrive not as a handful of scruffy fish bums who talk endlessly of fly patterns and bug hatches as they bump along in a rickety old Otter piloted by a mean-eyed little Frenchman chain-smoking unfiltered cigarettes and brooding over his unfaithful wife, but as one of four-score and seven Vacationing Professionals wearing the height of Friday-Is-Casual-Day fashion and sipping champagne in the shipshape and Bristol-fashion cabin of an Air Canadian 737.

You can almost believe you're in for a normal Northland experience when you touch down on the gravel runway carved from endless taiga and lined with landing markers made from yellow plastic shortening buckets, but this rustic illusion evaporates when you're whisked away to a spotless private cottage with maid service, thermostatically controlled heating, a bath with inexhaustible hot water, and a pot of decent coffee that arrives promptly at seven-thirty every morning. And the illusion is gone forever at mealtime, when the cavernous dining hall comes alive with uniformed young waitresses bustling to and fro with groaning trays of soup-to-nuts, and you spot a familiar face here and there in the crowd, including a mild-mannered Texan who summers in Maine and is accompanied by a small entourage of expressionless young men wearing wraparound sunglasses and talking furtively into their hands.

For those accustomed to the sporting North's usual rough-hewn squalor, Plummer's can come as a shock.

The first afternoon, after too much lunch and a brief indoctrination, we met our guides for the week and spread out across the lake in a flotilla of big aluminum skiffs, looking for Great Bear's major draw: lake trout.

In some circles it's fashionable to denigrate lake trout in general and trolling in particular, and while it's true that a lake trout is no match for a brown, rainbow, or brookie of the same size, it's also true that to the average Great Bear lake trout the average brown, rainbow, or brookie is little more than a light snack. And lake trout have their own brand of wild, lithe beauty, even a kind of senior-statesman majesty, for in the cold, infertile, almost tropically clear waters of Great Bear, where lake trout may grow only a half pound a year, a twenty-five-pounder is probably older than you are and a fifty-pounder is a Methuselah. And Great Bear has Methuselahs aplenty for anglers who stick with it.

Most of Plummer's guests do just that, dragging five-of-diamonds spoons the size of dinner plates endlessly around the lake, and they tot up amazing bags of fish—all but a few of which are released, I hasten to add. But any fish fights a dull, slogging battle with half a pound of metal stuck in its face. Catch them on a near-weightless fly, however, and lake trout become an entirely different creature.

Dease Arm, home to Plummer's Lodge since 1968, is comparatively shallow, and in the brief Arctic summer the trout hold mostly near the surface. If the caddis are hatching you can sight-cast to big lake trout with dry flies and emergers. But I was there late in the season and few flies were showing; if I wanted to catch lake trout I had to go dragging—and of course I didn't bring my regulation Maine salmon-trolling setup: a level eight-weight Cortland Super Sink with thirty-five feet of ten-pound Maxima. The Hi-D sink-tip I had along worked well enough for casual work, but if you mean to try for a big laker on a trolled fly you need the right stuff—something that will drag your fly down without dragging the fight from the fish.

With guide Matt Riger at the tiller and a short afternoon ahead, we sped south some fifteen miles to a cluster of small islands and cobble-bottom shoals that loomed up suddenly from the depths.

"What, about twelve, fifteen feet of water?" I said, watching a pair of dark, torpedic shapes swimming by slowly at what seemed, to my practiced nautical eye, only a few feet below.

Matt looked at the sounder. "No. More like forty-five or fifty."

Yikes. A whole new definition of clarity, and all the more reason to wish for a long, full-sink line to get the fly down where the big ones swim.

"Wadda they eat?"

"Oh, ciscos, grayling, smaller lake trout. A lot of sculpins, I think."

A little shy on grayling imitations, I knotted on a big weighted sculpin with Jitterbug wiggle-lips carved into its fat deer hair head, let out some seventy-five feet of line and thirty-five feet of leader, leaned back in the swivel chair, and fell into the somnambulistic underachiever rhythms of fly trolling. In a few hours I took half a dozen fat lakers between twelve and eighteen pounds—fish that initially came to the surface as meekly as a six-inch bullhead but which gained a whole new set of muscles and a dogged, head-shaking determination once they saw the boat, making run after run after run. And the best part was, in the perfectly transparent water I could see the whole fight taking place forty feet below. It was as though the world had inverted, with me at the bottom and the fish rushing and bulldogging high in the sky.

It's hard to imagine even the most cerebral fly fisherman spending an afternoon like that and still claiming with a straight face that lake trout aren't real fish and trolling with a fly isn't real fishing.

Still, I always feel vaguely uncomfortable unless I'm standing in running water, so the next day Matt and I headed thirty miles across the slick-calm lake to the Bloody River, where, he said, we might catch a few grayling.

With their trademark sailfish fin and thickly scaled, muscular bodies of green and silver with subtle touches of pink and red and electric blue, grayling are a good visual metaphor for the North: at first glance bleak and spare with an exaggerated topography, and on closer examination a complex mélange of textures and gay colors. As fighters grayling aren't in a class with trout, but they leap often enough and high enough to provide endless entertainment, they take flies readily, and they never, ever give up.

The Bloody is a small, bony river of bend pools and riffles surrounded by fields of cranberries and blueberries laced with bear and caribou trails. Using small Muddlers, Matt and I caught and released who knows how many grayling—the smallest around fifteen inches, the biggest just over nineteen, the majority around sixteen or seventeen. At breakfast the hardware anglers at my table had seemed amazed anyone would cross thirty miles of open water to catch sixteen-inch fish. "Fly fishermen," they'd said, elbowing each other knowingly, as though that explained any amount of moronic behavior.

Maybe it does, I thought, as we sat beside the idyllic little Bloody River, wondering about the origin of its name and eating grayling hot off an aromatic willow fire, watching eagles soar high overhead and listening, with that mixture of anxiety and anticipation peculiar to those eating fried fish in a bear-country berry patch, for that first inquisitive chuff.

The next morning found eight of us in a Cessna Caravan, faces pressed intently against the windows as we flew past sheer eroded cliffs and tablelands that looked lifted from a John Ford western, a scenic detour along the shores of Coronation Gulf. We turned at a broad estuary and headed south, and as the banks narrowed we got our first sight of the Tree River, for Arctic char anglers a true mecca. Lots of North Country water has Arctic char, but the Tree has *big* char, IGFA-record-class char. The previous night at dinner, that guy from Texas was telling us about a char his grandson, Jebbie, had tied in to—an easy twenty-five-pounder that had dragged him up and down the river for nearly an hour before finally squirting over a waterfall and breaking off.

For all its celebrity the Tree looks innocent and reassuringly intimate: Not much more than a long cast across, the Tree is about the size of the East Branch Penobscot or the Gallatin, though with a steeper, more anxious pitch and with that azure opalescence common to northern rivers busily buffing away at a landscape new and raw.

Plummer's camp at Tree, perched on the bank just below a booming set of rapids, is of the conventional North Country variety: hard-walled pipe-frame tents with a separate cookhouse and dining room and a couple of outhouses—a familiar and friendly environment, at least for those few of us in the scruffy fish-bum category; the Vacationing Professionals . . . well, they whined. No one listened to them, of course, for there were four or five miles of river to fish, with classic pools, long runs, and churning white water with tiny bankside pockets where, if you remained still and watched carefully, you could see fish cycling in and out of the current, catching a breath before heading on upstream to fulfill biological imperatives.

Arctic char are the perfect fish for the North. Big ones have the burning runs and athletic leaping abilities of Atlantic salmon, but instead of being tastefully appointed in princely silver and black, male char are a garish mixture of flame red and forest green— appropriate livery for fish living this close to Santa's workshop.

Fish are easily hooked on the Tree, but landing them is another matter entirely. The hardware anglers in our group seemed to be running around ten lost to one landed, and having left off complaining about the outhouses and mosquitoes were beginning to complain about all the six-dollar spoons they were losing. I did considerably better, which I of course attributed to my superior angling skills and the fly rod's efficiency as a fish-fighting tool, but which turned out to stem solely from the abrasion resistance of a fluorocarbon leader I'd brought along as an experiment. The first afternoon I hooked five fish, landing two pastel-green-dotted-with-pink-and-lavender hen fish of twelve and eighteen pounds, and technically landing a bright red male of around sixteen pounds. I say technically landed because the hook slid out at my feet as I fumbled with one hand for a camera and held the rod high with the other. Had I been less photographically intent I could have tailed him easily, but to what purpose? Why regret losing a fish mere seconds before I would have released him?

I do regret losing one fish—although I think it was Walton who said you cannot lose what you never had. I had been fishing an off-channel cul-de-sac known as the Presidential Pool, a favorite, they said, of that guy from Texas and Maine whose dog wrote that book and who has been coming here for years, but when it began to fill up with hardware anglers intent on fastening their spoons to the shallow bottom I headed downstream, looking for elbow room. While hopping from rock to rock I casually flipped a streamer into a dishpan-size pocket about ten feet away, and as I teetered around trying to regain my balance and save my hat from a sudden blast of wind, an enormous crimson char with lobster-claw jaws grabbed the fly, leaped head-high, and literally swam through the air, vibrating like a goldfish boosted from an aquarium. When he fell on the leader it cracked and whipped around my neck like a bullwhip. He had to weigh at least twenty-five pounds and maybe thirty, and if you ask me again in a year he may hit thirty-five, for as Saki wrote, "Freshwater fish and abnormal vegetables enjoy an afterlife in which growth is not arrested."

I lost the hat, too. Not to mention my only fluorocarbon leader.

The next morning, picking pockets along the bank as a damp gray miasma blew in off the Arctic Ocean, I started losing fish left and right. I did take three big whitefish in the eight-pound range, a ten-pound lake trout, and a twelve-pound hen char using a big black Zonker, and I lost another red of perhaps fifteen pounds that I had almost to the bank before he cut in his afterburners and rocketed straight through the haystacks in Class V white water faster than I could clear line.

"Wow, did you see that?" I asked an Inukshuk peering sympathetically down from the bench above. Conventional wisdom says the Inuit built these stone effigies everywhere they went as navigation beacons. But I think there's more to it than that. The Arctic is a lonely place, and no matter how far you've come or how bad things seem, the sight of a personable Inukshuk—a "semblance of man" in Inuktikut—always brings a smile.

One day on Great Bear, Matt and I were thirty miles south of the lodge, on a northern pike expedition to Cabin Bay, when a full autumnal gale blew down from the north and turned what had been a pleasant two-hour run down the lake into a scary backtracking five-hour slog into wind and rain. After hours of tacking back and forth across the wind, wet and cold and miserable, we happened upon a small island topped with the jauntiest, most cheerful Inukshuk imaginable. We landed there, happy to be off the pounding boat for a bit and hang out with an entity so anciently unflappable, and as we wandered around the little island the wind began to die and the rain petered out, and the remainder of our trip back to the lodge was peaceful and calm, and delightfully garnished by a big red-fin lake trout that struck a shallow-running streamer almost in the Inukshuk's shadow.

It was a pity the weather flushed us away early from Great Bear's primo pike hole. In the short time we were at Cabin Bay I caught some nice little pike in the six- to ten-pound range. As I levered a six-pounder to the surface, a dark Mesozoic shape some five feet long followed it up and lay awash alongside the boat, finning patiently and looking like something from which Johnny Weiss-muller might need to rescue Maureen O'Sullivan. When I worked loose the Mickey Finn and the little pike headed for the weeds, the monster followed it ponderously down, but whether as wolf or shepherd we could not tell.

"Pike," wrote Samuel Hearne, "are also of an incredible size in this extensive water; here they are seldom molested, and have mul-titudes of small fish to prey upon. If I say that I have seen some that were upwards of forty pounds weight, I am sure I do not exceed the truth." I'd say that was an understatement.

After a weather-aborted attempt the day before, on my last day we finally made it to the Coppermine River, flying in an Otter along the route north from Great Bear that Hearne, Franklin, and Richardson had followed. It took them two weeks; us, two hours. Cutting through a mile-wide valley surrounded by a high plateau, its banks steeply pitched and boulder-strewn, the Coppermine's broad riffled surface looked like a computer-enhanced version of the Yellowstone at Buffalo Ford; it may be the most beautiful spot I've seen in the North, or anywhere else, for that matter.

Compared with those of the Tree, the Coppermine's char run much smaller, but there are many more of them. The hardware guys in our group had a field day here, bombing out spoons and grinding in eight-pound char on nearly every cast. My fly rod and I had a much harder go of it, for there's little cover against the bank on the Coppermine and the fish lie much farther out than in the Tree. Meaning, of course, that there just had to be a twenty-five-knot headwind and no way for a sorry caster like me to get much farther out. Still, the Coppermine was generous enough, and I managed three nice silver hens and two dozen or better grayling up to a record-book-class twenty-two or so inches.

Again I lost a good red at bankside, but this time I wasn't scrabbling for a camera but gawking at a musk ox snuffling and grumbling his way up the bank an easy double haul away. But I was happy enough, for as I watched him plodding out of sight around the bend, I thought the scene a good trade for a fish I'd not intended to keep anyway, a fitting companion for the memory of that big Tree River char vibrating in the sun, for the lingering taste of a shore lunch featuring char cooked three ways—the best of which was not cooked at all but merely sliced thinly from a char's fresh quivering back—and for the sight of two white wolves I saw watching Plummer's Lodge early one morning from across the bay, waiting for fall to clear out the people and their noise so they could dine unmolested on the thick camp-follower population of marmots and hares grown porcine on handouts from Vacationing Professionals, themselves swollen with prime rib and three kinds of pie.

18

Ungava Ungawa

The land becomes large, alive like an animal;
it humbles him in a way he cannot pronounce.
It is not that the land is simply beautiful but
that it is powerful. Its power derives from the
tension between its obvious beauty and its
capacity to take life. Its power flows into the
mind from a realization of how darkness and
light are bound together within it, and the
feeling that this is the floor of creation.

—BARRY LOPEZ, *Arctic Dreams*

Trout fascinate anglers because trout live only in beautiful places. To me, brook trout live in the most beautiful place of all: the great untracked wilderness stretching from Newfoundland to Hudson Bay and north to the Arctic Circle.

So when Montreal-area outfitter Sammy Cantafio told me one winter that the Lefevre River, a small stream near one of his Arctic caribou camps, "has the largest concentration of speckled trout I've ever seen in all my years in the North," I got interested. And when he said, "It's only fished maybe once or twice a year, and then only in a few spots; some stretches have *never* been fished, and it runs through as wild a country as exists," I became obsessed.

This isn't a new obsession. When my boyhood friends were reading Blackhawk Comics and the Hardy Boys, I had my nose buried in everything I could find by Jack London and Robert W. Service, in Ernest T. Seton's *Rolf in the Woods* and *Two Little Savages*, James O. Curwood's *Kazan*, Bertrand Sinclair's *North of Fifty-Three*, John Rowlands's *Cache Lake Country*, Thoreau's *The Maine Woods*, Elliott Merrick's *True North*, and especially a book called *Traplines North,* the true account of a family of Canadian trappers who walked the winter wild on snowshoes and ate frozen mashed potatoes and moose meat and brook trout cached trailside in lard cans; I checked this book out of the elementary school library so many times a concerned librarian warned my mother I might be planning to run away from home.

Obsession? When my friends were playing Jackson at Chancellorsville or Mosby in the Valley, or Sitting Bull and Custer or Cochise and Jeffers, I was playing Hearne and Tyrrell exploring the wild Northlands, dreaming of caribou and Inuit, musk oxen and polar bears, birch-bark canoes and wigwams.

So it's no wonder that the August after Sammy triggered my latest round of North Country obsession, I found myself pressed against the window of a FirstAir 727, watching the trees disappear and the tundra unfold en route from Montreal to the Inuit village of Kuujjuaq, some 50 miles up the broad Koksoak River from Ungava Bay, just above fifty-eight degrees north.

The plan was for me to spend a few days at Sammy's caribou camp on Lake Napier, about sixty-five miles west of Kuujjuaq, sampling the brook and lake trout fishing and poking around the tundra, then fly into a wide spot on the Lefevre River with guide Chris Turcotte. Chris and I would float downriver in an inflatable for three days, fishing the "never been fished" rapids and pools and camping as the urge hit us. Then we'd hike a mile or so to the caribou camp at Lake Sabrina, spend the night, and fly back to Napier or one of Sammy's eleven other camps for a few days more fishing. "Weather permitting, of course."

Of course.

From the air the tundra looks culinarily creative—a stiffly beaten spice-cake batter swirled through with thin streaks of dull green and aquamarine and great irregular spatters of midnight-blue frosting. But as we nose down and glide into Lake Napier the land unfolds into a soft-focus rainbow. Millions of particolored wildflowers fleck a green gruel of peat and feathery lichens smeared thinly across glacial detritus. Tiny twisted willows and dwarfish spruce crouch in wind-sheltered folds—a Zen bonsai garden built by a small-town garden club with only a vague idea of the original.

Lake Napier is a perfect crystalline hourglass glacier-gouged into a setting of Precambrian gneiss. Seven miles long and over a hundred feet deep in places, Napier's shallows usually swirl with brookies herded there by the huge predatory lake trout that haunt its depths—two forty-pounders were taken here just last year. But in this summer of unrelentingly freakish weather, Saharan heat and a withering southerly wind have driven the fish deep, and we—camp manager Richard Woodland, Sammy's majordomo Bucky Adams, and I—manage only a few dozen brookies and lakers to six pounds or so over a few days of lazy, feet-on-the-gunwales fishing, as unlike the conventional Far Northern sport-fishing image as could be imagined. Replace our bug jackets with straw hats and garland the sparse willows with Spanish moss, and we could be characters from Uncle Remus.

On one uncharacteristically energetic day Richard and I head downlake to Napier's outlet, a narrow split in the ancient bedrock that jets icy water and forms a perfect plunge pool, deep and green and boulder-filled. Brookie after brookie chase my big windblown skater across the backswirling eddy like bored cats after a scurrying mouse. I release a dozen averaging eighteen inches and then lose count. The last and best fish Richard spots from the cliff above, and he semaphores my casts to its lair against the sheer rock wall. It's a splendidly fat and dramatically kyped twenty-two-inch male dressed in his spawning suit of flame red, his mouth spilling a squirming gout of stoneflies as I twist the skater from his jaw.

Early one morning Bucky's remarkably ursine snoring becomes a trombone duet, and we awake to find a young black bear staring in the camp window, sniffing at our bacon and butter and moaning to Bucky like a long-lost lover. Later, after the universally understood snick-snick-*git* of Richard's slide-action .280 sends him packing, I head for the outhouse and find a second, much larger set of tracks and a huge bear turd right in front of the outhouse door.

Returning from a two-mile hike into a voluptuous trout-filled lake that, Richard says, has no name and which I insist be ever after called Veronica Lake, after another boyhood obsession, we find a large wolf track overlapping our trail.

Late one night I hike up the ridge to the tablelands high above camp, where the unfettered wind holds briefly at bay the uncountable zillions of ravening mosquitoes working the night shift and I can pee in peace. A fat cheesy moon hangs low in the pale southern sky, and from it the sinuous swirl of the northern lights spirals out across the heavens. A wolf howls in the distance, and two Arctic foxes ghost by in the eerie green gloaming, not ten feet away.

This is the wild I've lived my life to find.

*   *   *

The next morning I'm in Sammy's Cessna, headed for the Lefevre with Chris, a North Shore Quebecker whose English is thankfully better than my uncouth phrase-book French.

Sammy buzzes the river before landing, and it looks perfect—easy stretches of rapids connect large, lakelike pools that glitter like disco domes countersunk into the broad green barrens. As we pitch the tent, clouds of caddis and mayflies pop rhythmically into the air, and stout black stoneflies scurry up streamside boulders.

Within a few hours Chris and I each take some four dozen gaudy, bull-strong trout between two and four pounds from the stair-step rapids near our tent. This is wild trout fishing as the first Europeans found it throughout North America, before short-sighted idiocy and unrestrained human reproduction destroyed irreplaceable habitats and whole populations of fish. Here at the extreme northern edge of the brook trout's range, the land remains undisturbed, truly virgin, and the fishing is nearly so.

It's too easy, really. A Muddler trailed inartistically in a current seam will catch every fish in a pool, one after the other; it's no more challenging than fishing a hatchery run. But I'm really here less to mindlessly catch fantastic numbers of wild speckled trout than simply to experience a land where fantastic numbers of wild speckled trout still exist. A land where there are more bears than people, where at any moment Ungava's million-strong herd of migratory caribou might top a nearby rise, clacking and shambling across the tundra, or a solitary musk ox loom from the mist that is part water vapor, part blackflies and mosquitoes.

At daybreak it's blowing southeasterly fifteen to twenty-five knots and raining hard. We break camp and load the boat—a hard-bottom inflatable dinghy designed to zip through smooth water propelled by a small outboard while carrying little more than an elegantly suntanned yachting couple wearing their drip-dry best to a pierside Caribbean jump-up. But we have miles of windswept currentless flatwater and thin bony rapids ahead of us, and we have only teaspoon-size oars with which Chris, perched precariously atop a wobbling mound of garbage-bag-swaddled equipment and provisions, barely makes headway against the wind.

Things are turning weird quickly. Last night Chris's ancient automatic fly reel ground to a halt and I loaned him my seven-weight, which promptly broke at the tip as he dragged a big trout up a run, leaving me facing miles of unfished wilderness river armed with nothing more formidable than a seven-foot three-weight I'd brought along as a lark.

The boat is clearly not up to the task, and neither is much of the rest of the gear, it seems—bought at the last minute for a trip theoretically planned six months before but now seemingly done on a whim, a trip that, as Chris adds ominously, has never before been done.

"Cantafio: 'e's big wit' concepts; not so big wit' details."

Chris mutters on, only part of which I understand: "Map? Map? Dere no fockin' map? *Merde!*"

Rain slashes us continuously. Heavy rain, light rain, but always rain. All day we are in continuous motion—me bailing, Chris rowing. I whine constantly about the weather, about my fly rod, about the laughably inappropriate boat, and the atmosphere become bitter and glum. Then Chris begins humming a sprightly air.

"That sounds familiar. A song handed down from the voyageurs, eh?"

"Non non non. Da theme to ah drim ov Jeannie."

We collapse in hysterics—two TV children of The Sixties, Gilligan and the Skipper in an inflatable *Minnow,* inching through a screaming storm in the wild Arctic barrens.

Our laughter seems to lift the clouds, and as we pinwheel out of control through the next rapids the sun burns through, the sky turns flinty blue, and the wind hauls swiftly into the northwest. We nose into the bank, and I step ashore onto a rock the size of a Thanksgiving turkey that promptly sinks like the proverbial stone and takes me with it into quicksand up to my naughty bits. I fling myself backward into the river and flail at the water, then Chris grabs my arm and I scramble back onboard, both of us still laughing like lunatics. We feel our way into a bight downstream that, after cautious probing, seems willing to hold our weight.

Chris heads up on the bench to make camp, and I confront the Lefevre's most difficult angling challenge: catching four ten-inch trout for supper. In an hour I release better than three dozen brookies between a foot and a half and two feet long, the fierce Arctic sun spotlighting their broad red sides as they twist and writhe like models on a runway. Finally, two eighteen-inchers driven mad by the Muddler take it so deep they virtually kill themselves, and I slice off pumpkin-orange fillets while Chris coaxes a willow-twig fire to life.

Stuffed with ambrosial trout and crisp-fried potatoes and onions, we crouch over the fire and smoke ourselves like bacon, growing a rind against the relentless assault of mosquitoes, an assault that, in the Arctic, ends only with the sudden onset of winter.

Dawn brings hard white lines rushing us-ward from a rust-streaked iron sky. We've both spent enough time in the North to know what this means: Winter's in a hurry this year. Time to head downriver. Fast.

While breakfast cooks I quickly catch a half-dozen more brookies, including a furious hook-jawed male of around six pounds that snaps at my hand like a bluefish, his white-tipped carmine fins flaring like matador capes as tries his best to smash my toy three-weight and its ridiculous little pepper-grinder reel.

This river is an improbably fertile strip cutting through an aggressively infertile landscape. Ropes of algae cover the shallows, fueled by the nitrogenous legacy of the millions of geese that raised their young here this summer and are even now heading south, straining Vs in the hard metallic sky. Insects grown fat on the bird-crap-fueled forage hatch continuously. The trout are broad-shouldered and wild as tigers.

The *Minnow* again sets sail, and after eight long hours of baling and rowing and singing sitcom theme songs and laughing maniacally through constantly contrary winds; after dragging the boat through half a dozen rapids and losing and finally recapturing an oar; after cowering in the willows as thunder crashes over our heads and lightning strikes all around us; after looking long and hard for a place to do the one thing no bug-jacketed visitor to the Arctic ever wants to do but inevitably must: lower his pants and squat—the trick is to sprint toward a sandy windswept hilltop absolutely devoid of vegetation and hope nature takes its course before the buzzing cloud of blackflies and mosquitoes sweeping back and forth across your scent trail like sharks running up a chum slick catches up and feasts on things best left unfeasted on. After all this, Chris finally begins seeing familiar scenes, and after rounding up above a falls and pulling hard against both the wind and a building current into the shelter of a well-willowed cove, we beach the *Minnow* like shipwreck victims, stuff essential gear into garbage bags tied together like hobo bundles, heave them across our shoulders, and strike off cross-country into the tundra, laughing and speculating about the oil stove's dry heat and the wondrous meal we'll eat tonight.

After a mile or so we reach Lake Sabrina and drop our loads; Chris hikes around the lake for the camp boat and I stumble back to the castaway beachhead for another load of stuff. We'll come back tomorrow for the rest of it, Chris says. Weather permitting, of course.

Sabrina turns out to be a disaster area. Chris says he's supposed to start rebuilding it this week, armoring its rattling pipe-frame tents with the stout plywood sides and layer of bubble-cap Mylar insulation that make Napier so snug; there'll be a generator and electric lights, a water pump, a bearproof combination storage and shower room. An Otter was to have brought in all the building materials and, more important, a luxurious cache of food. Weather permitting, of course. And of course weather didn't permit.

And visitors had been here before us: A pair of bears, the negative images of their dental work gnawed into every surface, had ripped into the tent and eaten most of the scant store of provisions and half the mattresses; big hunks of bear-mouth-shaped foam are everywhere. We go outside and look at the lowering clouds, get on the shortwave radio and talk things over with Sammy and Bucky back in Kuujjuaq. A huge low is moving in off Hudson Bay, they tell us, and we're gonna be here a while.

We're not laughing anymore. Gilligan and the Skipper may have fared just fine on their uncharted tropic isle, but we're in the Arctic, and the SS *Minnow* had an inexhaustible well of resources. Not to mention the Movie Star and Mary Ann.

And there's another crisis: In a few short hours Chris will be out of cigarettes, and I left my stack of books back at Napier. Soon, two addicts will be without a fix.

We had hoped, like Tolstoy's Platon, to lie down like stones and rise up like new bread, but morning brings more rain, freshening winds from the northeast, and a plummeting thermometer.

"How's the weather?" I mumble into the pale gray dawn from the depths of my sleeping bag.

"C'est juste de la merde," Chris growls. Everything is just shit.

Screw rising; there's no coffee anyway. We both turtle back into our bags and try to hibernate, an understandably popular pastime for weather-beleaguered tundra mammals.

Later we don foul-weather gear and hike back to the boat to paw through the remnants of food. We salvage a mold-flecked salami and a small chunk of ham, a pound of butter, half a bag of crushed oatmeal cookies, a handful of onions, a half jar of instant coffee, a rusty can of milk, two loaves of damp bread, a package of water-soaked spaghetti, six precious eggs.

We talk constantly of food, and the shortwave chatter brings vicarious thrills: Shirley way up at Helen's Falls salmon camp is making roast turkey and cheesecake. Daughter Marlene at the Weymouth Inlet char camp is fixing stuffed pork chops and lemon pie. We're having brown sugar on buttered toast and pondering the edibility of a Toronto-canned brand of meatballs that lists under its ingredients every known species of domestic animal separated by *and/or.* If the weather lets up, Chris says, we can hike four miles up to the next falls and catch some more trout, and we can take out his .22 and poach some ptarmigans. If the weather lets up.

Four days pass, four days of metering out morsels and listening to the relentless rain and howling wind, of trying to sleep through the shotgun blasting of tattered tent sides, of huddling next to the feeble oil burner wearing all our dirty laundry and exhausting the possibilities of multilingual conversation, of Chris longing for cigarettes and me for my new Cormac McCarthy sitting unread on a shelf at Napier, of listening to the constant Northland chatter over the shortwave, of wondering whether the bears will come back. Swaddled in oilskins, Chris digs a new garbage pit, polices the landscape for litter left behind by a winter's worth of vandalizing bears, loudly sings the Doors' "Riders on the Storm" in English and a bottomless supply of sixties sitcom ditties in French, over and over and over again. I scribble in my notebook and stalk the sodden ridges, squinting into the wind and hoping for a glimpse of caribou or musk oxen or bears or wolves—or a break in the weather.

Finally the wind drops and the skies clear, and we hear from Kuujjuaq that the Otter is on its way. An hour later, Chris smoking like the Marlboro Man, we've unloaded the lumber and food and propane, and I'm in the right seat headed for Kuujjuaq then Montreal.

Back home in Maine, as my sodden gear drying around the office emits the haunting, acrid smell of willow smoke, I look to the north and remember a land of terrible beauty. I think of bright flashing fish leaping in the low Arctic sun, and calculate the financial sacrifices I'll have to make to ensure my return, for return I shall. Weather permitting, of course.

Till then I can only dream, a starry-eyed romantic in the grip of Arctic fever, and sing the song of the North, a song as permanently imbedded in my psyche as the scent of willow smoke and the strong pull of wild trout:

Le Gilligaaaan, le Capitaaain, le Millionaaaire, son et Poooooooooooo.

19

A Proper Toff

*A knowledge of good form is prima facie
evidence that that portion of the well-bred
person's life which is not spent under the
observation of the spectator has been worthily
spent in acquiring accomplishments that are of
no lucrative effect.*

—THORSTEIN VEBLEN,
The Theory of the Leisure Class

In addition to disturbing insights into the Puritan mind, my brief
marriage to a Boston Brahmette with Pygmalion inclinations
left me with a passion for nineteenth-century British literature and
passing acquaintances with the arts of urbane conversation, sniffing
wine corks, and navigating superfluous tableware.

Eventually her relentless 'enry 'igginsing wore us both out, but
had I known how useful that thin appliqué of Beacon Hill social
graces would be on a fishing trip some quarter century later I'd
have stuck around another year and taken notes.

I knew it wasn't just any fishing trip when the theme from *Masterpiece Theatre* began blaring from my intracranial Victrola immediately upon turning off the road from Aberdeen to Balmoral, dodging pheasants and rabbits and roe deer and beech trees as old as the Battle of Bannockburn as I cruised the length of a long, wandering drive before finally docking at a compact Georgian mansion afloat in a sea of daffodils alongside Scotland's Royal River Dee.

Mouret's "Rondeau" was still playing as I knotted my tie and headed for dinner down a skylit circular staircase lined with stags' heads, Italianate statuary, and ancestral portraits that, were he wearing a flowing coiffure from the age of Dryden, Purcell, and Led Zeppelin, would look remarkably like John Foster, the present Laird of Park and our gracious host for a week of salmon fishing.

I tried not to look and sound too much like Gomer Pyle as I chatted with English guests wearing breeks and tweeds and golleed my way around the dining room and its graceful Adamesque fireplace topped by oils of Venetian fishermen toasting an eye-fluttering belle and before and after scenes of a typical British walloping of the Napoleonic fleet, its matched pair of oak-and-gilt moon-phase clocks still keeping perfect time more than two hundred years after their manufacture, its floor-to-ceiling French windows neatly framing the rushing Dee and its romantic backdrop of snow-crested mountains, before finally taking my seat at a massive mahogany table inset with a tapestry dating from that candlelit era when a lady's proper pastimes comprised needlework and swooning.

After a leisurely dinner, a touch of the floor-mounted bell summoned an effervescent Scots lass to clear away the remains of wood-pigeon breasts and Stilton-stuffed mushrooms and bring us another bottle of excellent claret to accompany the cheese-and-biscuit tray with its orbiting pair of porky little Norfolk terriers trying to cadge a bite of Gloucester Blue.

As I looked around, my internal trumpets still playing ruffles and flourishes, I thought Garn! Loverly! Ah-ah-ow-oo! After twenty-five years of hiding out in the Maine woods I have finally become a proper toff.

Sunday is a nonfishing day in Calvinist Scotland, but the river was nearby and beckoning, so after dinner we strolled down and found the Dee running high but well down from its bank-busting levels brought on by last week's Old Testament-tribulation rains. As we stood looking out across the peat-stained swirls a splendid salmon rolled, its broad side burnished brass by the last rays of the sun.

That image must have swum through our dreams, for the next morning we hardly touched breakfast, quickly donning waders and woolens against the chill drizzle oozing in off the North Sea and waddling off to the river as excited as children on Christmas morning. And why not? From its marches with Crathes Castle to its boundary some three miles downstream, the thousand-acre Park Estate spans some of the Dee's best water and, being the first real fishing above tidewater, offers Park's rods first refusal on every salmon to enter the river. The best of its twenty-one named pools, and arguably the best spring pool in all Scotland, is Park Inn.

Certainly the Old Major believed so. If he could fish only one pool, he was fond of saying, it would be Park Inn, this for its consistency and not just because it presented him with the forty-two-pounder hanging in Park's snooker room. Everyone speaks of the late Major Foster with reverence and more than a little awe. The Old Major shot five days a week and, in the March-through-September season, fished an hour and a half every morning and an hour and a half every evening. He was among the last of his kind:

aristocrat, autocrat, relentlessly enthusiastic sportsman of the Old School, and an inspiration to those of us who aspire to a life of sporting leisure but, through an unfortunate choice of parents, can only hire the experience by the week.

I headed upstream to try the sweeping Upper Kirks pool with head gillie David Bain, who pointed out the lies, rigged a fifteen-foot ten-weight, and gently tweaked my primitive colonial Spey-casting skills until I could roll the heavy Waddington halfway across the river into the teeth of a stiff breeze at least as often as I wrapped myself around in fankles and bugger's muddles.

Fishing down through the Upper Kirks, I soon fell into the easy rhythmic waltz of salmon fishing with a two-hander—lift load CHUCK drift, step-step; lift load CHUCK drift, step-step—the whole hypnotic dance accompanied by the rusty-hinge rasping of pheasants seeking mates beneath the yellow-blooming gorse, the coo-coo-cooing of amorous wood pigeons trysting in the pines, and the syncopated crump of censorial twelve-bores booming in the distance: a proper Fantasia for Sporting Gentlemen.

Even with a two-hander shouldering much of the load, fishing these high spring waters approximates actual work, with none of that effortless Arthur Wood-style drifting of feathery classic salmon patterns that characterizes the sweet days of summer. In April's frigid spates, you need to dredge bottom with a heavy full-sink or sink-tip line and big tube flies that look like feathered plumbing fittings if you're to goad a cold indifferent salmon into striking.

My first day I found them all indifferent and thought the river had gone fishless, but when David came in the Land Rover to collect me for lunch and we stopped to get Paul Tibbetts, woolgathering in the Long Pool, a large cock fish leaped sky-ward not twenty feet off his rod tip, and he was so startled he nearly swallowed his pipe.

We saw fish throughout the day, but they chose to ignore us. Still, everyone seemed happy and cheerfully optimistic at day's end, at least until our English guests heard that two French gentlemen fishing the opposite bank had caught a pair of nice salmon. Ah, the French and the English. Now, as in Henry V's time, their "very shores look pale with envy of each other's happiness."

With the weather beginning to clear from the northwest, Tuesday showed promise, but as we grew into our lives as Country Gentlemen we lingered long over the *Times* and a proper Scots breakfast: bacon and sausage and blood pudding and eggs, sautéed mushrooms and grilled tomatoes and real Scots porridge that is to American oatmeal what *Suprêmes de Volaille à Brun* is to Chicken McNuggets. As Dr. Johnson wrote of his trip through the Highlands, "If an epicure could remove by a wish, in quest of sensual gratifications, wherever he had supped he would breakfast in Scotland."

Paul wandered in late, muttering apologies as he straightened his tie and scraped marmalade across toast. He had gone stalking at daybreak and had seen eight deer, passing up a shot at a small roe buck in velvet and missing one large buck that, as he said, failed to oblige him by standing still. He and his hunting mate Barry Mordue planned a day of rough-shooting the vast flocks of wood pigeons ravaging the estate's newly sprouted oats and the battalions of Beatrix Potter-looking bunnies gnawing on everything else. Inspired by their industry, Peter London, Lawrie Hickman, and I pried ourselves from the *Times* and its Wettest-April-Ever headlines and headed for the Dee.

A few scattered March Browns were just popping off and random rises dimpled the surface, and Lawrie and I each caught a small brown trout in Park Inn. Then I fished Long Pool and Upper Kirks without a touch while with an equal lack of success black-and-white oystercatchers poked around the shallows with their crimson bills, and black-headed gulls flew up from the coast to see if the floods had canceled or merely rescheduled the ordinarily huge annual hatch of March Browns for which we all seemed to be waiting.

Even without the floods, fish runs were down. On the Dee as elsewhere, salmon struggle to survive human abuses of watersheds and high-seas refuges, not to mention centuries of the aristocracy knocking a hundred fish a day on the head and wondering, over brandy and cigars, where all the salmon have gone. Like many of the old ways, these attitudes are passing into history as reality bites hold of new generations, and catch-and-release, or at least very limited-kill, becomes more a necessary conservation measure than a conspicuous act of sportsmanship. This is especially true along the Dee, which alone among Scotland's four major salmon rivers—Dee, Tweed, Spey, and Tay—is fly-fishing-only.

I had begun to wonder if only the two French gentlemen across the river and the estuarine drift-netters who commercially vacuum up half of Scotland's annual salmon run could catch Dee springers, when toward evening Lawrie took a bright ten-pounder from the Cellar Hole and shortly afterward a twelve-pounder from Durris Stream. I found this both encouraging and discouraging, as except for the one little trout I had not yet touched a fish.

Wednesday blew in with more wind and rain; the river rose thirty-two inches overnight and showed enthusiasm for more. It was tempting to lounge on the drawing room Chesterfield with my feet to the grate reading Trollope, but the honor of the Colonies had to be maintained.

Although the river raged, I inched my way up its learning curve after getting two lackadaisical pulls from a nice fish that had spent the morning porpoising alongside one of the bankside daffodil

clumps the Old Major planted to mark the best lies. And I briefly
had hold of a fish of maybe ten pounds before trout-fishing the fly
right out of its mouth—making, as Jock Scott wrote, the "dreadful
mistake of raising the rod when you see the rise" instead of recit-
ing God Save the Queen as a gentleman ought.

I wasn't the only visiting angler with more to learn. A young
osprey whose eyes were bigger than his talons dove on a grilse that
promptly angled into the swift current and sent them both
hurtling downstream; by the time the bird finally jettisoned cargo
and lumbered into the air he was so far down on his Plimsoll he
looked like a periscope.

The rain built through the afternoon, washing out the fishing
and making the nightly British tradition of pub-crawling seem
more attractive than forting up alone in the drawing room with
Plantagenet Palliser and Lady Glencora. After dinner we all drove
upriver to the village of Kincardine O'Neil and the Gordon Arms,
a refreshingly untouristy little hotel and public house across the
road from what remains of the fourteenth-century Kirk of St.
Mary's after the Reformation finished reforming it.

The swirling mixture of Highlands Scots and Midlands English
grew ever more difficult to follow as various social lubricants did
their jobs, although the edgy sniping humor between conquerors
and conquerees was plain enough to a Southerner who had lived
long among the Yankees. Only Scotland and England suffered not
one but a seemingly endless string of bloody civil wars, all followed by cruel interludes of repression that make our own grim
Reconstruction seem like a cakewalk in the park. Then local
farmer Murray Brown told a story that smote a common foe and
reunited the kingdom: It seems a Deeside gillie known for his
uncommunicative ways was attending a patronizingly wealthy
German angler who lorded over the dim provincials his wide
travels and experiences with the world. When he turned to his

gillie, after an especially bombastic Teutonic harangue, and demanded, "My God man, have you ever even been off this estate?" the gillie said, "Just the once: 1939 to 1945."

When Burns wrote that "It's hardly in a body's pow'r, To keep, at times, frae being sour," he must have been looking out over a landscape much like the one framed by my bedchamber window the next morning. Rain had fallen throughout the night, flushing into the Dee the last of the mountain snows and enough brown peat to stuff every flowerpot in Edinburgh. With the house embayed and the river a foot over its gauge and rising fast, fishing seemed more than ordinarily pointless, so Lawrie and I decided to spend the day motoring about the Highlands, heading past the queen's digs at Balmoral and the Disneyland castle at Braemar for Grantown-on-Spey and Tomintoul, the highest town in Scotland. Murray calls it the town of creaky necks, from the villager's habit of sitting on their stoops watching openmouthed as cars go by, but with all the rain they could only peer suspiciously at our English license plates from behind half-drawn curtains.

We stopped at Abelour and watched a clutch of sodden anglers tossing prawns into the rain-swollen Spey, then we wandered about Grantown-on-Spey, a Victorian watering hole once on par with Ste.-Moritz, and found on display in Mortimer's angling shop books by John Gierach and Darrel Martin, further proof of the internationalization of angling.

We drove—or perhaps more accurately hurtled, as Lawrie is an ex-racing driver who enjoys what in the MG-TD days was known as enthusiastic motoring—past lonely grouse moors and roaring mountain burns, then we spiraled down through the lush Glenlivet estate with its vast shoals of pheasants and sheep wandering back and forth across the narrow twisting lanes and their infrequent enthusiastic motorers.

Except for a few widely scattered towns and great estates, the Highlands are today inhabited by little more than grouse and deer and sheep. Endless sheep. Countless sheep. Sir Walter Scott's heather-covered hills of "frowning defiance" have become Robert Louis Stevenson's "Hills of sheep, and the howes of the silent vanished races, And winds, austere and pure."

It's easy to see why tens of thousands of Highlands Scots, forced off their small farms by larcenous landowners clearing the way for wool and wealth, took to the mountains of North America: Round a bend and you're in the White Mountains, round another and you're in the Blue Ridge, and yet another and you're approaching the Front Range. And it's ironic that the exiled Highlanders prospered in the New World in ways they might never have done at home. Today the Highland clearances can be taken as a good thing or a bad thing, depending on how you feel about the class system and unpeopled wilderness, not to mention Campbell's Soup and McDonald's hamburgers.

Friday, with signs of clearing and the river down nearly five feet from its crest last night, I tied on a Gold Willy Gunn and headed for the Cellar Hole, where I finally caught my first Dee springer— "fresh run, blue-green and silver bright," as Scots novelist Neil Gunn wrote in *Highland River*, "and of all shapes surely the most perfect in creation." Fortunately for me and my winter-rusted fish-fighting skills, this lively ten-pounder decided his best escape was to swim upstream; within five minutes he was landed, tagged, and released, but not before becoming, as gillie Keith Cromar said, "the most photographed bloody fish in Scotland."

The westerlies built to gale force throughout the afternoon and fishing became increasingly an exercise in frustration, but the next morning, with the river perfect, the wind low, and the sun bright, I took another ten-pounder from the Cellar Hole and shortly after, near a plaque commemorating Bonnie Prince Charlie's stopping for a drink during his flight into exile after the Forty-Five, caught a strong twelve-pounder from Durris Stream; five times I fought him to the bank and five time he dashed off before gillie Alastair Friend finally slipped a net under his head.

For the week eleven fish went to six rods, but three were Lawrie's and three were mine, and upon my sworn oath that I had none but English and Scots ancestors this was deemed an event worth celebrating in the old way, so back at the fishing hut we poked up the fire, sat down with local salmon aficionado and raconteur David Egan, and toasted the salmon and the river and each other from silver cups filled with *aqua vitae, uisge beatha,* water of life, Famous Grouse.

Underlying the auld ceremony was a bit of hair-of-the-dog, for we—meaning Lawrie and his friend Alison, and Murray Brown and his wife, Carol, and David Egan and his wife, Ella, *Trout and Salmon's* irrepressible Deeside columnist—had until the wee hours shot snooker at Park, expounding on world affairs and deciding that poachers and game hogs and drift-netters and myopic politicians and environmental despoilers should all simply be taken out and shot. And we had, of course, done justice to Park's wine cellar, as proper toffs are wont to do.

I hated to see my week at Park as a Gentleman of Leisure come to a close, but there was a bright spot: The next day Lawrie and I were headed across the Grampian Mountains to Dunkeld to sponge off his friend John Derricott for a few days. John had prime fishing at his Stenton Manor on the Tay, Lawrie said, not to mention a fine little loch filled with brown trout and a good nose for wine.

I was learning fast. And this time I was taking notes.